Henry Stanley
and the European Explorers of Africa

General Editor

William H. Goetzmann
Jack S. Blanton, Sr., Chair in History
  University of Texas at Austin

Consulting Editor

Tom D. Crouch
Chairman, Department of Aeronautics
  National Air and Space Museum
  Smithsonian Institution

WORLD EXPLORERS

Henry Stanley
and the European Explorers of Africa

Steven Sherman

Introductory Essay by Michael Collins

CHELSEA HOUSE PUBLISHERS

New York • Philadelphia

On the cover 16th-century map of Africa; photograph of Stanley from *The Autobiography of Henry Morton Stanley*, courtesy of the Library of Congress

Chelsea House Publishers
Editorial Director Richard Rennert
Executive Managing Editor Karyn Gullen Browne
Executive Editor Sean Dolan
Copy Chief Philip Koslow
Picture Editor Adrian G. Allen
Art Director Nora Wertz
Manufacturing Director Gerald Levine
Systems Manager Lindsey Ottman
Production Coordinator Marie Claire Cebrián-Ume

World Explorers
Senior Editor Sean Dolan

Staff for HENRY STANLEY AND THE EUROPEAN EXPLORERS OF AFRICA
Copy Editor Margaret Dornfeld
Editorial Assistant Robert Kimball Green
Picture Researcher Wendy Wills
Senior Designer Basia Niemczyc

First printing

1 3 5 7 9 8 6 4 2

Library of Congress Cataloging-in-Publication Data

Sherman, Steven.
Henry Stanley and the European Explorers of Africa / Steven Sherman.
p. cm.—(World Explorers)
Includes bibliographical references and index.
Summary: A history of the European exploration of Africa, focusing on the work of Henry Stanley.
ISBN 0-7910-1315-4
　　0-7910-1544-0 (pbk.)
1. Stanley, Henry M. (Henry Morton), 1841–1904—Juvenile literature. 2. Explorers—Africa, Sub-Saharan—Biography—Juvenile literature. 3. Africa, Sub-Saharan—Discovery and exploration—Juvenile literature. [1. Stanley, Henry M. (Henry Morton), 1841–1904. 2. Explorers. 3. Africa—Discovery and exploration.] I. Title. II. Series.　　　　92-31066
DT351.S9S55 1993　　　　　　　　　　　　　　　　　CIP
916.704'32—dc20　　　　　　　　　　　　　　　　　　AC

CONTENTS

WORLD EXPLORERS

THE EARLY EXPLORERS

Herodotus and the Explorers of the Classical Age
Marco Polo and the Medieval Explorers
The Viking Explorers

THE FIRST GREAT AGE OF DISCOVERY

Jacques Cartier, Samuel de Champlain, and the Explorers of Canada
Christopher Columbus and the First Voyages to the New World
From Coronado to Escalante: The Explorers of the Spanish Southwest
Hernando de Soto and the Explorers of the American South
Sir Francis Drake and the Struggle for an Ocean Empire
Vasco da Gama and the Portuguese Explorers
La Salle and the Explorers of the Mississippi
Ferdinand Magellan and the Discovery of the World Ocean
Pizarro, Orellana, and the Exploration of the Amazon
The Search for the Northwest Passage

THE SECOND GREAT AGE OF DISCOVERY

Roald Amundsen and the Quest for the South Pole
Daniel Boone and the Opening of the Ohio Country
Captain James Cook and the Explorers of the Pacific
The Explorers of Alaska
John Charles Frémont and the Great Western Reconnaissance
Alexander von Humboldt, Colossus of Exploration
Lewis and Clark and the Route to the Pacific
Alexander Mackenzie and the Explorers of Canada
Robert Peary and the Quest for the North Pole
Zebulon Pike and the Explorers of the American Southwest
John Wesley Powell and the Great Surveys of the American West
Jedediah Smith and the Mountain Men of the American West
Henry Stanley and the European Explorers of Africa
Lt. Charles Wilkes and the Great U.S. Exploring Expedition

THE THIRD GREAT AGE OF DISCOVERY

Apollo to the Moon
The Explorers of the Undersea World
The First Men in Space
The Mission to Mars and Beyond
Probing Deep Space

CHELSEA HOUSE PUBLISHERS

Into the Unknown

Michael Collins

It is difficult to define most eras in history with any precision, but not so the space age. On October 4, 1957, it burst on us with little warning when the Soviet Union launched *Sputnik*, a 184-pound cannonball that circled the globe once every 96 minutes. Less than 4 years later, the Soviets followed this first primitive satellite with the flight of Yuri Gagarin, a 27-year-old fighter pilot who became the first human to orbit the earth. The Soviet Union's success prompted President John F. Kennedy to decide that the United States should "land a man on the moon and return him safely to earth" before the end of the 1960s. We now had not only a space age but a space race.

I was born in 1930, exactly the right time to allow me to participate in Project Apollo, as the U.S. lunar program came to be known. As a young man growing up, I often found myself too young to do the things I wanted—or suddenly too old, as if someone had turned a switch at midnight. But for Apollo, 1930 was the perfect year to be born, and I was very lucky. In 1966 I enjoyed circling the earth for three days, and in 1969 I flew to the moon and laughed at the sight of the tiny earth, which I could cover with my thumbnail.

How the early explorers would have loved the view from space! With one glance Christopher Columbus could have plotted his course and reassured his crew that the world was indeed round. In 90 minutes Magellan could have looked down at every port of call in the *Victoria*'s three-year circumnavigation of the globe. Given a chance to map their route from orbit, Lewis and Clark could have told President Jefferson that there was no easy Northwest Passage but that a continent of exquisite diversity awaited their scrutiny.

In a physical sense, we have already gone to most places that we can. That is not to say that there are not new adventures awaiting us in the sea or on the red plains of Mars, but more important than reaching new places will be understanding those we have already visited. There are vital gaps in our understanding of how our planet works as an ecosystem and how our planet fits into the infinite order of the universe. The next great age may well be the age of assimilation, in which we use microscope and telescope to evaluate what we have discovered and put that knowledge to use. The adventure of being first to reach may be replaced by the satisfaction of being first to grasp. Surely that is a form of exploration as vital to our wellbeing, and perhaps even survival, as the distinction of being the first to explore a specific geographical area.

The explorers whose stories are told in the books of this series did not just sail perilous seas, scale rugged mountains, traverse blistering deserts, dive to the depths of the ocean, or land on the moon. Their voyages and expeditions were journeys of mind as much as of time and distance, through which they—and all of mankind—were able to reach a greater understanding of our universe. That challenge remains, for all of us. The imperative is to see, to understand, to develop knowledge that others can use, to help nurture this planet that sustains us all. Perhaps being born in 1975 will be as lucky for a new generation of explorer as being born in 1930 was for Neil Armstrong, Buzz Aldrin, and Mike Collins.

The Reader's Journey

William H. Goetzmann

This volume is one of a series that takes us with the great explorers of the ages on bold journeys over the oceans and the continents and into outer space. As we travel along with these imaginative and creative journeyers, we share their adventures and their knowledge. We also get a glimpse of that mysterious and inextinguishable fire that burned in the breast of men such as Magellan and Columbus—the fire that has propelled all those throughout the ages who have been driven to leave behind family and friends for a voyage into the unknown.

No one has satisfactorily explained the urge to explore, the drive to go to the "back of beyond." It is certain that it has been present in man almost since he began walking erect and first ventured across the African savannas. Sparks from that same fire fueled the transoceanic explorers of the Ice Age, who led their people across the vast plain that formed a land bridge between Asia and North America, and the astronauts and scientists who determined that man must reach the moon.

Besides an element of adventure, all exploration involves an element of mystery. We must not confuse exploration with discovery. Exploration is a purposeful human activity—a search for something. Discovery may be the end result of that search; it may also be an accident, as when Columbus found a whole new world while searching for the Indies. Often, the explorer may not even realize the full significance of what he has discovered, as was the case with Columbus. Exploration, on the other hand, is the product of a cultural or individual curiosity; it is a unique process that has enabled mankind to know and understand the world's oceans, continents, and polar regions. It is at the heart of scientific thinking. One of its most significant aspects is that it teaches people to ask the right questions; by doing so, it forces us to reevaluate what we think we know and understand. Thus knowledge progresses, and we are driven constantly to a new awareness and appreciation of the universe in all its infinite variety.

The motivation for exploration is not always pure. In his fascination with the new, man often forgets that others have been there before him. For example, the popular notion of the discovery of America overlooks the complex Indian civilizations that had existed there for thousands of years before the arrival of Europeans. Man's desire for conquest, riches, and fame is often linked inextricably with his quest for the unknown, but a story that touches so closely on the human essence must of necessity treat war as well as peace, avarice with generosity, both pride and humility, frailty and greatness. The story of exploration is above all a story of humanity and of man's understanding of his place in the universe.

The WORLD EXPLORERS series has been divided into four sections. The first treats the explorers of the ancient world, the Viking explorers of the 9th through the 11th centuries, and Marco Polo and the medieval explorers. The rest of the series is divided into three great ages of exploration. The first is the era of Columbus and Magellan: the period spanning the 15th and 16th centuries, which saw the discovery and exploration of the New World and the world ocean. The second might be called the age of science and imperialism, the era made possible by the scientific advances of the 17th century, which witnessed the discovery of the world's last two undiscovered continents, Australia and Antarctica, the mapping of all the continents and oceans, and the establishment of colonies all over the world. The third great age refers to the most ambitious quests of the 20th century—the probing of space and of the ocean's depths.

As we reach out into the darkness of outer space and other galaxies, we come to better understand how our ancestors confronted *oecumene*, or the vast earthly unknown. We learn once again the meaning of an unknown 18th-century sea captain's advice to navigators:

> And if by chance you make a landfall on the shores of another sea in a far country inhabited by savages and barbarians, remember you this: the greatest danger and the surest hope lies not with fires and arrows but in the quicksilver hearts of men.

At its core, exploration is a series of moral dramas. But it is these dramas, involving new lands, new people, and exotic ecosystems of staggering beauty, that make the explorers' stories not only moral tales but also some of the greatest adventure stories ever recorded. They represent the process of learning in its most expansive and vivid forms. We see that real life, past and present, transcends even the adventures of the starship *Enterprise*.

To Timbuktu and Back

In the heat of the day of June 28, 1796, the Scottish explorer Mungo Park climbed a tree to get a better look at where he was going. He hoped, from his elevated vantage point, to spy some huts, cattle, even a plume of smoke, anything that would indicate human habitation of the empty spaces that stretched out before him to the horizon, but he saw only "the same dismal uniformity . . . of thick underwood and hillocks of white sand." He descended, removed the bridle from his horse to lighten its load, and laid down in the burning sands of the Sahara Desert. Unbearably thirsty, sick and delirious, he thought to himself (he wrote later), "Here then, after a short but ineffectual struggle, terminate all my hopes of being useful in my day and generation. Here must the short span of my life come to an end." During his yearlong quest to reach the Niger River and the legendary city of Timbuktu, Park had often been in danger—menaced in warring kingdoms, robbed, enslaved, starved—but never before had he abandoned hope. He tried chewing the leaves from some shrubs to slake his thirst, but they were bitter and offered no relief. All around him, "the burning heat of the sun was reflected with double violence from the hot sand," and far off "the distant ridges, seen through the ascending vapour, seemed to wave and fluctuate like the unsettled sea." He prepared to die.

He came to in the cool of the evening, sufficiently restored to attempt to press on. With his horse, too weak to carry him, plodding along ahead, he moved slowly

Alone, ill, starving, robbed of his possessions, the Scottish explorer Mungo Park many times had reason to fear for his life in the course of his first expedition in search of the Niger. Nevertheless, he persisted, and "in the stirring history of African exploration," according to the British historian E. W. Bovill, "there was no more dramatic event than [Park's] discovery of the Niger."

forward. After an hour, lightning began to flash in the distance, and a strong wind started to rage. Anticipating rain, Park expectantly stuck out his tongue, only to have it and the rest of his body "instantly covered with a cloud of sand." The relentless sandstorm lasted an hour.

The storm ended, and he continued onward. Once again lightning lit the sky, and he disrobed and spread his clothing out on the ground. The rain fell for hours, and Park drank by wringing the water from his drenched clothing and even sucking on the wet cloth. Daybreak found him near some muddy pools filled with frogs, whose croaking had guided him through the darkness. They were so numerous and so loud that his frightened horse would not approach the water to drink until Park had scattered them by thrashing about with a branch. Then he climbed another tree and this time saw, unfurling against the merciless sky of the desert morning, a wisp of smoke from a native village several miles away.

Mungo Park's foray in search of the Niger was the first manifestation of a renewed interest on the part of Europeans in the geography and exploration of Africa, a renewal that would culminate in the highly publicized explorations of the journalist and adventurer Henry Stanley in the latter part of the next century. The first era of European interest in Africa, in which the most significant explorations were conducted by sea along its coasts, primarily by Portuguese mariners in the 15th and 16th centuries, had left as its most significant legacy the commerce in the continent's dark-skinned native peoples as slaves. In the new era that Park helped usher in, the focus would be on overland explorations of the continent's interior—most particularly the courses of its mightiest rivers, the Nile, the Niger, the Congo (referred to sometimes as the Zaire), and the Zambezi—and the consequences for the native inhabitants of Africa would be no less momentous.

There were several reasons for Europe's renewed interest in Africa. During the earlier era, the slave-trading nations had done little more than build fortresses and outposts along Africa's West Coast (especially in the lands adjoining the Gulf of Guinea) and wait for chieftains from the interior, who were eager to obtain such European manufactured goods as beads, woven cloth, and firearms, to send them slaves. The interior went largely unexplored by Europeans, in part because of the obstacles to travel presented by climate, terrain, and the hostility of native peoples but mainly because with trade so lucrative on the coast, there seemed to be little additional profit that could be gained inland. All that the Europeans wanted in trade from Africa—slaves, gold, silver, ivory, various agricultural products—could be obtained on the coast.

By contrast, the primary impetus for the inland exploration of Africa by Europeans was the emphasis in the late 18th century—a period of time historians call the Enlightenment—on science and empirical knowledge. During this time of scientific discovery, geographical exploration, and economic expansion, the absence of even the most basic information about the great continent to Europe's south was seen as an embarrassment by many of the learned men of the age. To most Europeans, Africa was little more than a dark, ominous shape on the map below the Mediterranean, home only to exotic wildlife, impenetrable, steaming jungles, and savage tribesmen. Next to nothing was known of its history, its peoples, its cultures, or even of the existence, location, and nature of its most dominant geographic features, a dearth of knowledge satirized by the great 18th-century Irish poet Jonathan Swift, who wrote, "So Geographers in Afric-Maps / With Savage-Pictures fill their Gaps / And o'er unhabitable Downs / Place Elephants for want of Towns." Even so outstanding a geographical feature as the Niger River, which was hundreds of miles longer than any watercourse in Europe or North America (but was still, behind the Nile and the Congo, only the third longest on the so-called Dark Continent) was little more than a rumor; even the most accomplished cartographers and scholars in Europe knew neither its source, its outlet, or even the direction of its current. Likewise the precise location of the storied city of Timbuktu, long the center of the African gold trade and thus synonymous for centuries in the European mind with mysterious wealth, remained unknown.

In England, especially, this want of knowledge was regarded as an embarrassment. There, in 1788, at a London tavern called the St. Alban's, Sir Joseph Banks—famous naturalist, president of the Royal Society (the nation's preeminent scientific organization), and companion of Captain James Cook on that estimable mariner's first circumnavigation of the world—and nine of his learned and wealthy colleagues formed the African Association. "So

Sir Joseph Banks, president of the Royal Society and founder of the African Association, first achieved fame as an explorer and scientist through his service with Captain James Cook's first Pacific expedition. "Though we have been ignorant since the revival of letters, that this river existed," read the minutes of an early meeting of the African Association, "it was known to the Ancients by the name of Niger. . . . In what manner this river disembogues itself is not known."

long as men continued ignorant of so large a portion of the globe, that ignorance must be considered as a degree of reproach on the present age," read the founding resolution. "That as no species of information is more ardently desired, or more generally useful, than that which improves the science of Geography; and as the vast continent of Africa, notwithstanding the efforts of the Ancients, and the wishes of the Moderns, is still in great measure unexplored, the members of this Club do form themselves into an Association for promoting the Discovery of the Inland Parts of that Quarter of the World."

The group's interests soon focused on the exploration of the Niger. When the first explorer they sent out to ascertain the character of the great river, James Houghton, was robbed and then killed by the native inhabitants of the hinterlands between the Senegal River and the Niger, in what is present-day Mali, the association began looking for another adventurer to penetrate the interior. In Mungo Park, a young Scottish physician hungry for fame and willing, he said, to go "to Timbucktoo and back" to attain it, the association believed they had found the man for the job.

Park was born in 1771 in the hilly countryside outside of the Scottish town of Selkirk. His parents, intent on securing the best possible future for their 12 children, had them privately tutored in their crowded three-room farmhouse. Young Mungo loved ballads and stories of ancient times; once he complained bitterly to a servant who was sweeping up some loose pages of an old book that she was destroying literature. "It's just Old Flavel," she replied, to which he instantly retorted, "Ay, you or somebody else, you will one day be sweeping up my book leaves saying they were old Mungo Park's." His greatest joy was rambling about the countryside alone, and from a young age he exhibited a desire for fame mixed with an equally strong taste for solitude—a seemingly perfect combination for an explorer.

Park's father, a tenant farmer, wished him to become a clergyman, not out of any special feeling of piety but because a clerical post was a good way to advance in the world, but at age 15, Park chose instead to study medicine and was apprenticed to Dr. Thomas Anderson. Three years later, he went to study at the University of Edinburgh, where he developed a taste for botany and gained a reputation as a hard worker.

Park then traveled to London, where his brother-in-law James Dickson was a well-known botanist. Dickson introduced him to Joseph Banks, who found Park a job as assistant surgeon on an East India Company ship bound for Sumatra, a large Indian Ocean island southeast of the Malay Peninsula that is today one of the principal parts of the nation of Indonesia. The healthy crew required few of Park's medical skills, but he distinguished himself nonetheless by studying the biology and natural history of the area, documenting eight new species of fish. Banks, impressed by his work, decided that the 24-year-old Park was just the individual for the African Association.

Park's mission was simple. He was, instructed the association, "to ascertain the course and, if possible, the rise and termination of the River Niger . . . and use his utmost exertion to visit the principal towns or cities in its neighbourhood, particularly Tombuctoo and Hausa." His motivation for undertaking such a hazardous enterprise was equally straightforward, as he explained in a letter to one of his brothers: "If I succeed I shall acquire a greater name than any man ever did!" He believed as well that he owned all the qualifications necessary to succeed in this undertaking: "I had a passionate desire to examine . . . a country so little known. . . . I knew that I was able to bear fatigue, and I relied on my youth and the strength of my constitution to preserve me from the effects of the climate."

After a voyage of a month aboard a trading vessel bound for Gambia from Portsmouth, Park arrived at Jillifree, a West African port on the northern bank of the Gambia

River, in late June 1795. There he met and was befriended by Dr. John Laidley, an English slave trader at whose home in Pisania, farther inland on the Gambia, he was to spend much of the next six months while organizing his expedition. Most of that time was spent attempting to gather information about the peoples of the interior, such as the Mandingoes and the Fulani; Park had been able to gather only the sketchiest of details from the handful of Europeans who had traveled inland. The *slatees*, or black merchants, whom he spoke with after his arrival in Africa proved to be unreliable; uncertain of his motives, and not eager to provide knowledge that might enable Europeans to make direct contact with their trade sources in the interior, the slatees purposefully fed the inquisitive Scotsman misleading and contradictory information about the people and places farther east. Park was able, while in Pisania, to learn enough of the Mandingo language to communicate successfully. He also experienced a portent of things to come when a severe tropical fever laid him low for several weeks.

With the arrival of the dry season, in early December, Park set out, accompanied by Johnson, a black servant who spoke both Mandingo and English, and Demba, a slave provided by Laidley who spoke the interior languages and had been promised his freedom should he serve Park well. Madibo, a black freeman; Tami, a blacksmith; and two slatees offered their services until they reached their destination of Bondu, a region to the northeast of the Gambia. Park's small party also had a horse, two donkeys, and a modest amount of baggage: "a small assortment of beads, amber and tobacco, for the purchase of fresh supply . . . a few changes of linen, and other necessary apparel, an umbrella, a pocket sextant, a magnetic compass, and a thermometer, together with two fowling pieces, two pairs of pistols and some other small articles." Although he was setting forth in tropical West Africa, Park dressed as if he were in Scotland, in a long, heavy coat and a wide hat.

His journey first took him east, through forested, gentle
hills with towns set in the valleys, to Medina, the clay-
walled capital of the kingdom of Wooli, where he arrived
on December 5. He generally enjoyed the week that he
spent in the kingdom, where he noted in his journal such
Mandingo pastimes and institutions as wrestling matches
and Mumbo Jumbo, a disguised figure who beat women
whose husbands complained about them ("a strange bug-
bear . . . much employed by the pagan natives in keeping
their women in subjection" in Park's own words). One local
custom—that of hanging colorful rags or pieces of cloth
from the branches of a large tree to mark one's passing and
propitiate local spirits—charmed him greatly, and Park
added a swath of colorful cloth to the tree. "I cannot . . .
take leave of Wooli without observing that I was well
received by the natives, and that the fatigues of the day
were generally alleviated by a hearty welcome at night, and
although the African mode of living was at first unpleasant
to me, yet I found, at length, that custom surmounted
trifling inconveniences, and made everything palatable
and easy," he wrote.

Park also enjoyed his travels through Bondu, largely
populated by the light-skinned Fulani, an Islamic people
whom Park described as naturally mild and gentle but
hardened by the Koran, the sacred book of Islam. The
Fulani were herdsmen who "display great skill in the man-
agement of their cattle, making them extremely gentle by
kindness and familiarity." In Fatteconda, the capital city of
Bondu, the king's dozen wives greeted Park with hilarity,
poking fun at his pale skin and thin, prominent nose. "They
insisted both were artificial," Park wrote. "The first, they
said was produced when I was an infant, by dipping me in
milk, and they insisted my nose had been pinched every
day, till it had acquired its present unsightly and unnatu-
ral conformation." With the generally unflagging good
humor with which he would meet the travails of his journey, Park agreed with their assessment and complimented

Mungo Park's greatest virtue as an explorer was his stoical perseverance in the face of all manner of daunting circumstances, but this was not, ultimately, sufficient to bring him success. The words he penned in the course of his second Niger expedition proved prophetic: "Though all the Europeans who were with me should die, and though I were myself half dead, I would still persevere; and if I could not succeed in the object of my journey, I would at last die on the Niger."

their own beauty. Though discomfited, Park did not lose his temper when Almani, Bondu's king, pronounced himself dissatisfied with the presents—gunpowder, tobacco, and amber—that the explorer had given him in order to secure safe passage through his kingdom. The king wanted as well Park's blue dress coat with the yellow buttons; the Scotsman was assured, for his sacrifice, that Almani would wear the coat on all public occasions.

The adventurer and his tiny retinue had been traveling northeast since leaving Pisania, and on January 10, having crossed the Senegal River into the kingdom of Khasso, Park's small band arrived at Jumbo, Tami's hometown. The blacksmith received a jubilant reception from the inhabitants of his home village, leading a watchful

Park to conclude that "whatever difference there is between the Negro and European in the confirmation of the nose and the colour of the skin, there is none in the genuine sympathies and characteristic feelings of our common nature." At Koniakary, the kingdom's capital, the monarch tried to dissuade Park from traveling onward; all the adjoining kingdoms were soon to be at war with one another, said the king. A more immediate obstacle was the king's greed; he and his advisers helped themselves to all of Park's remaining store of trade goods.

The outbreak of war, Park learned as well, was also likely to mean the resumption of slave raids by the Moorish peoples to the north. When Park learned that the townspeople of Funingkedy, where he arrived on February 15, were planning to move en masse southward to Jarra out of fear of such attacks, he decided to join the exodus. Undeterred by Park's "protection," the Moors (the term is Park's imprecise, all-purpose description of any of the Islamic, Arabic peoples of North Africa) swept down on the town before it could be evacuated and made off with cattle and captives. When, as the only means of saving his life, Park contemplated amputating the infected leg of a young boy who had been shot in the raid, "this proposal made everyone start with a horror, they had never heard of such a method of cure and would by no means give their consent to it; indeed they evidently considered me a sort of cannibal for proposing so cruel and unheard of an operation." The Africans instead attempted to save the boy by whispering sentences from the Koran in his ear; he died that same night.

The hostilities left Park's companions fearful that they might be captured and reduced to slavery and extremely reluctant to carry on. Johnson decided to return to the coast, but Park succeeded in gaining permission from the representatives of Ali, the Moorish king of Ludamar, to pass through his kingdom, which the explorer estimated was 560 miles from his starting point. But Park was now traveling in regions whose inhabitants had never seen a white man, and Ali, in the person of eight horsemen, summoned the Scotsman personally to hot, barren Benown on the pretext that his wife wished to see a Christian. The summons left Park uneasy; he had already been abused and robbed by the Muslim inhabitants of Ludamar, and it was in this kingdom that Houghton had met his death. Although he was initially not treated badly at Benown—he was forced, however, to share his hut with a wild hog, his Islamic hosts' contemptuous allusion to Christianity's allowing its adherents to eat pork—Park remained fearful: "I was a stranger, I was unprotected, and I was a Christian."

Soon, his situation worsened. Demba was enslaved, and Park was often denied food, water, or permission to leave, though still ostensibly in possession of his freedom. His captors' hatred of Christians made him an outcast. One

This engraving was one of the illustrations in Park's narrative of his first Niger expedition, Travels in the Interior Districts of Africa.

man, about to give Park a drink, "recollected that I was a Christian, and fearing that his bucket might be polluted by my lips, he dashed the water into the trough. . . . Though this trough was none the largest, and three cows were already drinking in it, I resolved to come in for my share and kneeling down, thrust my head between two of the cows and drank with great pleasure." He was told each night that in the morning he was to be executed, until after some time the threatened punishment was lessened: Daybreak would bring, he was now informed, the putting out of his eyes because "they resembled those of a cat." "Never," wrote Park, "did any period of my life pass away so heavily; from sunrise to sunset was I obliged to suffer with an unruffled countenance the insults of the rudest savages on earth."

Eventually, Park was made to accompany Ali as he inspected his kingdom. At various outposts in the months of May and June 1796, Park was shown off as a kind of trophy. At Bubaker, he was nearly laid prostrate by the "insufferable" heat that blasted "the dreary expanse of sand, with a few stunted bushes and trees" that Park noted as the region's predominant landscape, where mangy goats and camels searched in vain for shade and foliage. There, too, he watched helplessly as Demba was formally sold into slavery. In Jarra, when Park overheard Ali's men talking about bringing him back to Benown, he decided to make his escape and slipped away on the night of June 28 on a stolen horse. Brandishing guns, a party of Moors on horse-back—Park feared they were Ali's men—overtook him at dawn, but they proved to be only bandits intent on steal-ing his cloak, which was the last of his possessions, aside from the tattered clothes on his back. Though his situation was certainly desperate—indeed, seemingly hopeless—Park felt as euphoric as "one recovered from sickness," and he rode on alone. That elation soon turned to despair as the barrenness of the scorched landscape impressed itself upon him. Horse and rider plodded onward in the shimmering, vaporous heat until Park at last halted, set the horse free, climbed a tree to reconnoiter the featureless horizon, concluded that he was to die, and sank acceptingly into the southern Sahara's indifferent sands, only to be saved by the night and the howling desert storm.

The smoke that Park had spotted from his treetop vantage point rose from a Fulani village. Near death, he made his way to this settlement, only to be turned away by its chief. Outside the village walls, however, an old woman took pity on the staggering, emaciated figure and fed him a meal and gave his horse some corn. The next day, after negotiating a rugged stretch of terrain overrun with wild boar, ostriches, and antelope, Park came upon a Fulani shepherd camped by a stream with a woman and three children. Park by this point had been reduced to crawling on his hands and knees; the shepherd also took pity on him and fed him, even though the explorer's confession that he was indeed a Christian sent the woman and children screaming from their hut in terror. (Muslim folklore in these parts held Christians to be monstrous beings capable of the most unspeakable behavior.) Similar acts of kindness sustained him over the next several days as he made his way to the village of Oussebou, where he arrived on July 7 and rested for four days.

Once sufficiently restored to travel, Park set out again, this time in the company of two guides. He was now moving southward; as he proceeded, he realized with mounting anticipation that the object of his quest—the Niger River, which the natives of Bambara, the region through which he was now passing, called Joliba, or the Great Water—was now not far off. On July 21, Park recalled later, "we rode together through some marshy ground, where, as I was anxiously looking around for the river, one of [the guides] called out 'Geo affili' (See the water). . . . I saw with infinite pleasure the great object of my mission, the long sought for majestic Niger, glittering to the morning sun, as broad as the Thames at Westminster and flowing slowly to *east-*

At Kamalia, Park recuperated from the travails of his first expedition. His recovery was aided by the kindness shown him by a slave dealer named Karfa Taura, who provided him with a hut, "a mat to sleep on, an earthen jar for holding water, and a small calabash to drink out of . . . [he also] sent me, from his own dwelling, two meals a day, and ordered his slaves to supply me with firewood and water."

ward." So was resolved the first of the great geographical riddles to puzzle the European explorers of Africa, but Park's success would ultimately only raise further questions.

His trip back to the coast was only somewhat less eventful than his trek to the Niger. He followed the river northeastward to Silla, intending to set out east from there to Jenne (present-day Djenne), a city on the Bani River, one of the Niger's many tributaries, but fever, exhaustion, and the loss of his overworked horse finally convinced him, on July 30, 1796, to turn back. Pelted by rain, menaced by the distant roar of lions, weakened by hunger, and robbed once again by bandits, his progress constantly hampered by flooding rivers and streams, he staggered into Kamalia, a Mandingo town on the Baoule River, a tributary of the Senegal, on September 30. He was filthy, jaundiced, emaciated, and ill and likely would have died were it not for the solicitude shown him by a slave dealer named Karfa Taura, who provided him with a hut and several substantial meals a day. "Thus was I delivered, by the friendly care of this benevolent negro, from a situation truly deplorable," wrote Park.

During his convalescence in Kamalia, Park studied the town in detail, recording his observations on everything from marriage customs and laws to the slave trade. Park spoke to the slaves whom Karfa Taura planned to take to the coast for sale and learned that "a deeply rooted idea is that the whites purchased Negroes for the purpose of devouring them," a fear common among slaves all over Africa. Though he expressed some sympathy for the plight of the captured, the Scottish wanderer concluded that "the effect (of abolishing the slave trade) would neither be so extensive or beneficial as many wise and worthy persons fondly expect."

Though Park's fever lifted with the end of the rainy season, he spent more than six months in Kamalia, waiting for Karfa Taura, whom he was going to accompany to the coast, to ready his coffle. (A coffle is a train of slaves fastened together for transportation, usually by chains or a wooden yoke.) In mid-April, coffle, slave trader, and explorer departed together, traveling westward toward and then along the Gambia through "woody but beautiful country, interspersed with a pleasing variety of hill and dale, and abounding with partridges, guinea fowls and deer." Along with the scenery, Park observed how an uncooperative slave woman was treated: She was repeatedly whipped and beaten, and then, when she became too weak to walk, placed upon "a sort of litter of bamboo canes . . . and tied with slips of bark." The next day, the slave traders attempted to tie her to the back of a mule, and when she slipped off, they cut her throat. Park reached Pisania, where he was reunited with Dr. Laidly, in mid-June; he departed on an American slave ship one week later

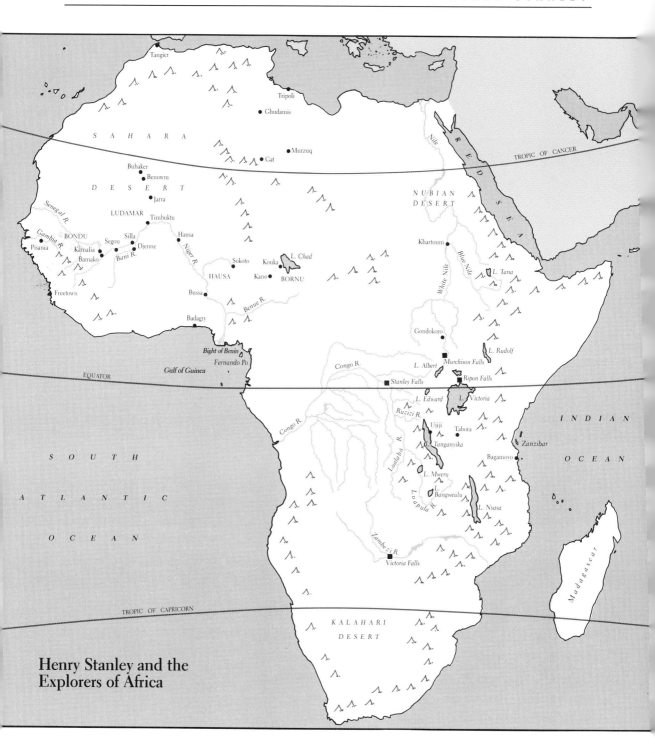

**Henry Stanley and the
Explorers of Africa**

and arrived finally in England on December 22, 1798, two long years after he had left.

But Park's belief that in reaching the Niger he would "acquire a greater name than any man ever did" was not to come true. The account he wrote of his journey—*Travels in the Interior Districts of Africa in the Years 1795, 1796 and 1797*, compiled from notes he had stored in the crown of his hat during his wanderings—was well received, and geographers and scientists pored over his findings, but his shy personality did not make for an imposing public presence, and those who met him in London society or heard him lecture generally found him insufficiently heroic in person for celebrity. In short time, he returned to Scotland, married Alison Anderson—"the lovely Allie," as he always referred to her—and started a medical practice in the town of Peebles. Domestic and professional life satisfied him for a while—he turned down an opportunity to lead an exploratory expedition in Australia—but soon he found himself yearning to return to Africa, which, despite all the hardships he had suffered, continued to exert an inexorable pull on him. He regarded his work there as unfinished, in that he had failed to reach either Timbuktu or the mouth of the Niger, and when the British government, intrigued by Park's accounts of commerce in gold and eager to keep the French out of the region, approached him about leading an expedition for that very purpose, he proclaimed that it would make him "the happiest man on earth" to undertake such a mission.

But Park's second expedition proved to be a disaster. He and his company left Pisania for the interior in the first week of May 1805, the hottest time of the year and just a few weeks before the onset of the rainy season. The 35 British soldiers who had volunteered for the expedition in exchange for double pay and a discharge of their remaining tour of duty proved, though they had been garrisoned on the coast, ill-suited for African expedition and unsuitably provisioned. Overloaded donkeys refused to work or, once the rains started, bogged down in the mud while the sol-diers, clad in red flannel uniforms and shouldering full military packs, quickly sickened and died in the 135-degree heat. Bandits regularly waylaid the expedition, tribal chief-tains demanded exorbitant tribute to pass through their territory, and hired porters pilfered provisions. "Loaded asses tumbling over the rocks, sick soldiers unable to walk, black fellows stealing," Park wrote about a typical day.

With June came the rains. Now "is the beginning of sorrow," wrote Park. "The rain had set in, and I trembled to think that we were only halfway through our journey. The rain had not commenced three minutes before many of the soldiers were affected with vomiting; others fell asleep and seemed as if half intoxicated." By mid-August, more than 30 of Park's party had perished. (There were, as well as the soldiers, Park's brother-in-law Alexander Anderson, an artist, several carpenters, a couple of sailors, a black African guide, and assorted attendants.) Those who remained were menaced by lions—the huge cats hunted and killed the donkeys in broad daylight—and hyenas and jackals, who scavenged around their camps at night, eyes glowing demonically in the light from the campfire. Isaaco, the guide, was badly injured by a crocodile that attacked him as he was fording a stream; he was able to keep the sharptoothed reptile from dragging him beneath the waters to his certain death by jamming his fingers in its eyes. Troops of bandits, their numbers greater than the ex-plorers', trailed the straggling column, awaiting the chance to make off with a pack animal or bundle of provisions.

By the time Park's expedition reached the Niger near Bamako (now the capital of Mali) in mid-August, only 12 of its original 45 members were still alive, and one of those was insane. Near Segu, Park and his soldiers fashioned a flat-bottomed craft from two derelict canoes given them by a sympathetic local ruler, and in this unlikely vessel, outfitted with a crude cabin, hide sails, and a hide shield around the deck, the explorers, their numbers now

Park meets his death in the Great Water near Bussa in 1805. Investigations by later explorers revealed that Park had taken a bellicose stance toward the native peoples along the Niger, refusing to pay tribute or parley with the chieftains along the way, which led to frequent skirmishes and ultimately his death.

reduced to just four, made their way downriver, Park himself navigating from the deck while wearing his "long coat, his straw hat, and large gloves," according to a later German journeyer who heard the account years afterward from some natives. There were occasional skirmishes with the inhabitants of the lands along the Niger's banks and a bloody confrontation with an enraged mother hippopotamus. Finally, at Bussa, some 1,600 miles downriver from his starting point but still 500 miles shy of his goal of the Niger's mouth, Park's long journey came to an end. Out of ammunition, on the verge of being overwhelmed by Hausa tribesmen, Park and the other surviving European member of his company, John Martyn, abandoned ship for the waters of the Niger and were immediately drowned.

The Bornu Mission

Despite Park's assertion, made despite the travails of his second expedition (the Scotsman's diaries and the recollections of Isaaco, who survived the disastrous journey, provided the basis for the posthumously published *Journal of a Mission to the Interior of Africa*), that merchandise could be safely and easily transported from the interior to the Gambia River with the loss of "not more than three or at most four men out of fifty," the failure of his attempt to reach the mouth of the Niger and chart its entire length and of several similar endeavors launched subsequently by the British created an interest in finding a new, presumably safer and easier route to the African interior.

When, in 1815, Great Britain resumed its exploratory efforts in Africa after a hiatus forced by its involvement in the Napoleonic Wars, from which it emerged as the most powerful nation in Europe, its attention became focused on reaching the Niger and Timbuktu from the north of Africa rather than from the west, specifically from Tripoli, a city (now the principal seaport of the nation of Libya) on the Mediterranean Sea where the British maintained a significant military and commercial presence. The words penned in 1817 by commander W. H. Smyth, a young naval officer stationed there—"I am becoming still more convinced that here—through this place, and by means of these people . . . is an open gate in to the interior of Africa"—found favor with John Barrow, founder of the Royal Geographical Society (RGS), which would oversee and underwrite much of the British exploration of Africa. (The Royal Geographic Society had in the meantime

This engraving of one of the bodyguards of Mohammed El Kanemi, sheik of Bornu, illustrated Dixon Denham's Narrative of Travels and Discoveries in Northern and Central Africa, *his account of his expedition to Bornu with Hugh Clapperton and Walter Oudney.*

Hugh Clapperton volunteered for the Bornu mission by pointing out that his previous service in the Royal Navy had "often brought me in contact with uncivilized tribes and in my intercourse I have always had the good fortune to insinuate myself into their good opinion." He would get along much less well with Denham, his colleague on the Bornu mission.

absorbed the African Association.) Barrow was among those who believed that the Niger—the entire length of which remained uncharted—joined at some point with the Congo or the Nile, and he believed an expedition overland to the Niger from the north would confirm his theory. Though the endless and unforgiving sands of the Sahara lay between Tripoli and the most likely destinations in the interior, the idea was that the explorers would use long-established caravan routes through the desert, where a local ruler, the Bashaw, who was well disposed toward the English, claimed that he could guarantee their safety.

Accordingly, in 1821 the British consul to Tripoli, Hanmer Warrington, began laying plans for an expedition into the interior to Bornu, a kingdom southeast of Lake Chad in the present-day country of Nigeria. Three ill-matched individuals were placed at the expedition's head: Walter Oudney, like Park a somewhat shy, young—he was 31 when the expedition departed Tripoli in 1822—Scottish physician with a keen interest in botany and the natural sciences; Hugh Clapperton, two years older, also a Scot, a handsome, outgoing career navy man; and Dixon Denham, a brave though disagreeable and arrogant army officer. Oudney and Clapperton were friends, but neither of them liked Denham, who reciprocated their feelings. The two Scotsmen were of a scientific bent and resented Denham's attempt to impose military discipline on the expedition; the Englishman, for his part, found his two colleagues "tiresome," "vulgar," and poorly prepared by character and experience for the undertaking. He fostered a special dislike for Clapperton, whom he found unbearably conceited (the feeling was mutual) and accused of a litany of faults and misdeeds, including a supposed love affair with his manservant. This quarrelsome trio was given a dual objective: Establish a British trade presence in Bornu while recording various geographical observations and discoveries made en route, including, it was hoped, the source of the Niger.

Dissension was evident from the outset. Oudney and Clapperton were already well on their way south to Murzuq, an oasis 500 miles south of Tripoli, when Denham finally set out in March 1822. While delighting in the friendly welcome he received in the towns along the way— "This to us, was highly satisfactory, as we were the first English travellers in Africa (from the north) who had resisted the persuasion that a disguise was necessary"— Denham characteristically slighted Oudney and Clapperton, who had, after all, passed through ahead of him, a tendency that would be evident throughout his published account of the Bornu mission, *Narrative of Travels and Discoveries in Northern and Central Africa.* (European travelers in Muslim lands, such as those of North Africa, had traditionally found it prudent to travel disguised as Arabs.)

At Murzuq, to their mutual dismay, the explorers were reunited. Some bad news worsened their distemper: The Bey of Fezzan, a local potentate who was to have guided them southward, had changed his plans and now could not set out for another 18 months. Denham took this opportunity to decamp back to Tripoli and then England, while Oudney and Clapperton decided to explore the desert as far west as the oasis and town of Gat, near the present-day border of Libya and Algeria. The magnificent desolation of the Sahara greatly impressed them: "The presence of nothing but deep sandy valleys and high sand hills strikes the mind forcibly. . . . Who can contemplate without admiration masses of loose sand, fully four hundred feet high, ready to be tossed about by every breeze and not shudder with horror at the idea of the unfortunate traveller being entombed in a moment by one of those fatal blasts?" At Gat, where they arrived on July 26, Oudney and Clapperton found the townspeople cheerful and friendly, but their excursion was not otherwise a pleasant one: When Denham returned to Murzuq on October 30, he found both men virtually prostrate with fever, though not too weak to express—in the form of indignant letters to Warrington—

their continued distaste for the Englishman, who had, however, succeeded in obtaining the services as guide of one Abu Bakr bu Khullum, a Fezzan "merchant of very considerable riches and influence in the interior." Bu Khullum was accompanied by a large retinue of perhaps as many as 200 Arabs.

Denham's return spurred the ailing Oudney and Clapperton to some semblance of vitality, and they departed Murzuq on November 19, ten days ahead of Denham and bu Khullum. Traveling on camels and horses, both parties passed through a lifeless desert lit by a burning sun and at night thousands of glittering stars. At Gatrone, the explorers reunited and continued southward through a nightmarish bare plain littered with the bleaching bones of slaves who had perished along this route on the way to Tripoli. On some, patches of skin and even facial hair were still evident, and the hooves of the horses and camels splintered and scattered the skeletons as the caravan passed through. The Arab members of the party showed scarcely more respect, casually insulting and cursing the souls of the dead slaves, replying to Oudney's protests that the corpses were merely those of black slaves. Once, a merchant traveling with the caravan suddenly exclaimed, "That was my slave. I left him behind four months ago, near this spot." "Make haste. Take him to the *fsug* [market]," retorted an Arab wag, "for fear anybody else should claim him." Hungry for amusement, some of the Arab camel drivers succeeded in capturing a live hyena, which they tied to a stunted tree and then blew to pieces with gunfire. Some days, sandstorms literally blotted out the sun, and a prickly grass tortured the men and the animals with what felt like the constant jabbing of dozens of small, sharpened needles. Oudney and Clapperton grew sicker and weaker, and soon Denham, too, was feeling ill. At one point, all the members of the caravan—man and beast—went eight straight days without water. On the first day of the new year 1823, the camels began to die.

Hardship created no bonds between the explorers. Clapperton steadfastly refused to obey the imperious Denham, who continued to issue commands nonetheless and responded to Clapperton's recalcitrance by writing scurrilous letters to Warrington about the Scotsman's alleged sexual misconduct. By the time the explorers reached the oasis of Bilma, in what is now northeast Niger, Clapperton and Denham were communicating with each other only in writing. The oasis did prove a welcome respite from the travails of their journey nonetheless—Denham characterized the local women, on whom he found "the pearly white of their regular teeth . . . beautifully contrasted with the glossy black of their skin," as "very seducing"—and on February 4, 1823, the explorers reached Lake Chad, a huge but extremely shallow body of water at the conjunction of the present-day borders of Chad, Niger, Nigeria, and Cameroon. According to Denham, the explorers believed the lake "to be the key to the great object of our search" in that a prevalent geographical theory held that the Niger terminated in the same inland lake—Lake Chad perhaps?—that was in turn the supposed source of the Nile. The explorers accordingly surveyed the shores of the

As night begins to fall, hyenas move in on a group of dying slaves, cut loose from their coffle because they were too sick to keep up. Denham, Clapperton, and Oudney would sometimes encounter the corpses of several hundred slaves in a single day.

The Fulanis at the town of Museifa hold their ground in the face of a charge by Bornu slave raiders accompanied by Denham and an Arab contingent. "The [Fulani] warriors were so thick that there was no standing against them and the Arabs quickly fell back," Denham wrote.

lake, looking for verification of this theory, which they believed they had found with their discovery, on February 14, of the Yobe River flowing eastward into the lake. This, the explorers, as well as their correspondent Barrow, initially took to be "unquestionably the Niger."

They would soon be disabused of this notion. While participating in a disastrous slave raid on the Fulani town of Museifa (some 200 miles south of the lake, in present-day Cameroon) with Bu Khullum and a contingent of Bornu men loyal to Sheik Mohammed El Kanemi—a shower of poisoned Fulani arrows left the marauders "a confused flying mass" that "plunged in the greatest disorder into that wood we had but a few hours before moved through with order and very different feelings"—Denham ascertained that there was no river flowing south from Lake Chad that could be the Niger. He also earned censure from Oudney—"the expedition failed at which none of us can be sorry, but rather rejoice that the cause of humanity has prevailed"—and British government officials for his participation in a slave raid. Unchastened, Denham, accompanied by Oudney this time, then helped El Kanemi put down an uprising in the rebellious province of Manga.

Such adventuring occupied the explorers until the onset of the rainy season, at which time they retired to Kouka (present-day Kukawa), the Bornu city where Clapperton had been convalescing, trying to shake the fever, chills, and coughing that had racked him since the outset of the journey. The coming of the rains laid Oudney low again as well; while the two countrymen shivered and sweat on pallets in a rude hut, tormented by the bites of scorpions

The title page and frontispiece to the first edition of Denham's narrative of the Bornu mission. The figure in the frontispiece is Mohammed El Kanemi, the so-called Sheik of Spears, who had won power in Bornu by leading a rebellion against the Fulani, who had temporarily seized control of the sultanate.

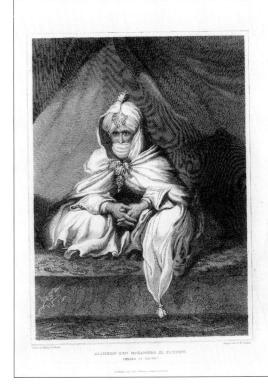

At Kouka (present-day Kukawa), the explorers met Ibrahim Lefiani, the figurehead mai, or sultan, of the province of Bornu. "He was seated in a sort of cage of cane or wood," Denham wrote, "near the door of his garden. . . . Nothing could be more absurd and grotesque than some, nay all, of the figures who formed this court." The mai ruled at the sufferance of Sheik Mohammed El Kanemi, who wielded the true power in Bornu.

and ants, their fever dreams punctuated by the nighttime laughter of hyenas prowling outside the town's walls, Denham explored the town, practiced his Arabic, and gathered more geographical information about the regions surrounding Lake Chad. By December, when the rains stopped, the two sick men were feeling better, which meant strong enough to separate themselves from Denham, and the Bornu mission split up once again.

Accompanied by Ernest Toole, an enthusiastic young army officer who had traveled from Tripoli to Bornu to join the explorers at Kouka, Denham moved southeast to survey further the area around Lake Chad, particularly the lovely Chari River. At a village called Angala, south of the lake, Toole died, apparently from malaria. Denham, who had at last found a friend in the Bornu mission, was distraught. Upon his return to Kouka, he learned that Oudney had met a similar fate at Katagum on the way to the province of Kano, which the two Scotsmen had set out to explore. Clapperton continued westward as far as Sokoto, a city and province on a tributary of the Niger (in what is now northwest Nigeria) into which he was escorted by an honor guard of 150 horsemen sent out to greet him by the Fulani potentate Sultan Bello, before returning to Kouka. From the sultan, Clapperton learned that the Niger flowed into the Atlantic, although the potentate later tried to recant this assertion by producing a map showing it coursing into the Nile. (The Niger does in fact flow into the Atlantic, but farther east in the Gulf of Guinea than the Bight of Benin, which is where Bello placed its mouth.) The two surviving leaders of the Bornu mission therefore returned to England in June 1825 more certain of where the Niger did not terminate—Lake Chad—than of its actual course. Denham clung to the theory that the Niger somehow joined with the Nile at some point, a theory that Barrow continued to espouse as well. Clapperton put his trust in the initial assertion of Sultan Bello that the river flowed into the Atlantic, while Oudney had met his death believ-

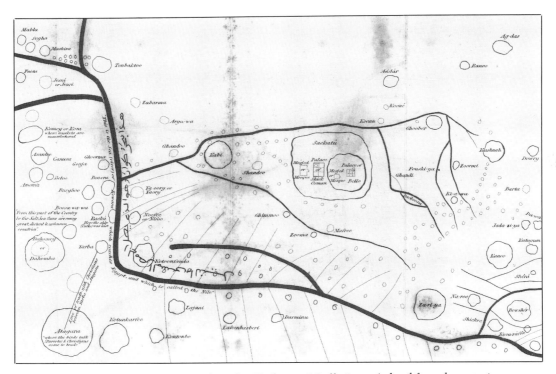

ing that the great river terminated in the "Lakes at Nyffe," a marshy region south of Sokoto.

Even so, the expedition marked a milestone in African exploration. Between them, Clapperton, Oudney, and Denham had mapped three sides of Lake Chad, determined the borders of desert, savannah, and forest in the region, pioneered a route for Europeans from North Africa to the central interior, surveyed much formerly unexplored territory, and established a British presence in areas where it had previously been unknown. Nevertheless, it was the mystery of the Niger that remained the immediate focus of the European exploration of Africa.

A detail from the map given Clapperton by Sultan Mohammed Bello, a Fulani ruler, that showed the Niger flowing eastward all the way to the Nile. In all likelihood the map was designed to misrepresent the Niger's course in order to dampen the enthusiasm of the English about using the river as an easy inroad to the interior.

The Niger
Riddle Solved

Even before Clapperton's return to England, another expedition had been dispatched from Tripoli for the purpose of reaching Timbuktu and ascertaining the course of the Niger. Its leader was Alexander Gordon Laing, yet another Scotsman. Laing, who was 32 years old, was a former schoolmaster who had abandoned education in favor of the adventurous life of a member of the Royal Africa Corps and earned promotion to major as the result of an exploratory journey in West Africa, in what is now the nation of Sierra Leone. He was then posted to Tripoli, where he had the good fortune to meet and marry Emma, the beautiful daughter of Hanmer Warrington, the British consul there and patron of exploration. In 1824, two days after his wedding, Laing set out from Tripoli for Timbuktu and the Niger. His course was to take him through the Sahara and the Sudan along caravan routes in a generally more westerly path than that taken by the Bornu mission.

Despite the travails that he had so recently endured, Clapperton arrived in England eager to return to Africa and resolve the mystery of the Niger, an intention that grew only stronger when he learned of Laing's mission. Accordingly, he spent only three months in England before taking ship for the Bight of Benin. There, from the port city of Badagry, he intended to travel overland to the river town of Bussa, on the Niger, visit Sokoto once more, and then

Richard Lander (seen here disguised as an Arab) came to Africa as Clapperton's servant on his second expedition, but he was to achieve fame in his own right. John Barrow, president of the Royal Geographic Society, wrote of him: "The long sought for termination of that river . . . called the Niger, has now been discovered, and by a very humble but intelligent individual, who . . . accomplished, not without difficulty and danger, an undertaking in which all former travellers had failed."

return to the river and follow it either to its source or its terminus.

The most important member of Clapperton's small party proved to be his personal servant, 20-year-old Richard Lander. Self-described as a man of "rambling inclinations," Lander, who was a native of Cornwall, cherished the ambition of learning about "the manners and ceremonies of the natives of distant regions of the world." Thus far, he had satisfied this aim by, as a very young man, hiring on as a sailor aboard a schooner bound for the West Indies and then as personal assistant to wealthy older men given to travel. When he heard of Clapperton's mission to "ascertain the source, progress, and the termination of the mysterious Niger," he quickly offered his services. "There was always a charm in the very sound of Africa," wrote the indefatigable Lander; "its boundless deserts of sand, the awful obscurity in which many of the interior regions were enveloped; the strange and wild aspect of countries that had never before been trodden by the foot of a European, and even the very failure of all former undertakings to explore its hidden wonders, united to strengthen the determination I had come to."

The Clapperton party departed from Badagry on December 7, 1825. In the early days of the journey, the company traveled through dense forests "wholly impenetrable by man or beast," according to Clapperton, except on the narrow trail on which they traveled. In the heavily populated region of Yoruba (in present-day Nigeria), the countryside grew "quite enchanting," hilly, with well-tended fields of corn and yams and many villages, where the explorers were greeted upon arrival with cries of consternation, as if, according to Lander, they were "wild beasts or monsters of some sort." Everywhere, however, the people were friendly, often escorting the wayfarers most of the way to the next village. Clapperton acquired a wife as a gift from a generous local potentate, and so, at Wawa, almost did Lander, though he was finally able to deflect the attentions of the widow Zuma—the owner of 1,000 slaves and the best house in town—to his master, "who made," he wrote, "my retreat as soon as I could, determined never to come in such close quarters with her again." Despite the merry widow's overfamiliarity, the travelers enjoyed Wawa, where, according to Clapperton, "the want of chastity and drunkenness" of the inhabitants generally made for an enjoyable stay.

The explorers arrived at Bussa, where Mungo Park had met his death on the Niger, on March 30, 1826, just ahead of the rains. Five members of the party had died en route, and Clapperton and Lander had both been intermittently ill; Clapperton at times had to be carried along on a litter, while Lander sometimes grew delirious and attacked his master. The rains laid both men low, and it was several weeks before they could set out to the northeast for Kano. In the interim, Clapperton questioned the chief at Bussa about the death of Park; although the man was reluctant to talk about the incident, Clapperton concluded that his fellow Scotsman had hastened his demise by his aggressive posture on approaching Bussa, for he found the Kambari people of Wawa and Bussa generally "mild" and "lazy . . . more stupid-looking than wild."

The illness of the two men persisted on their way to Kano, which they reached in July after much hard traveling through torrential rains and a storm-soaked, though beautiful, landscape of rich fields and pasturelands. Both men were now constantly burning with fever and had to be helped on and off their horses. Clapperton remained the stronger, and while Lander convalesced at Kano he continued on westward to Sokoto, where he was reunited with Sultan Bello, who welcomed him with the "utmost cordiality." The sultan once again provided the explorer with some new information about Africa, regaling him with tales of the cannibalism practiced by the Jacoba people to the north—"whenever a person complained of sickness among these men, they are killed instantly, for fear they

"The Bornu caravans never go farther than this place," Clapperton wrote about the marketplace at Kano. "The caravans from Cubbi, Youri, and Zamfra bring principally slaves and salt, which they exchange for natron, gora nuts, beads, horses, robes dyed of a dark blue, having a glossy and coppery tinge."

should be lost by death, as they will not eat a person who dies of sickness," claimed the sultan—while the Scotsman expressed disbelief.

Clapperton never got the opportunity to verify Sultan Bello's tales. Soon after Lander arrived in Sokoto in December 1826, his illness returned, and despite his servant's tireless ministrations, this time there was to be no recovery. He died on April 18, 1827, leaving Lander with specific instructions for the disposal of his effects and some general advice as to how to bring his journey to a safe conclusion: "Bear yourself up under all your troubles like a man and an Englishman; do not be afraid and no one will hurt you."

Whether Lander succeeded in banishing fright only he could say, but a succession of often terrifying circumstances forced him to disregard his master's advice to head for Tripoli rather than the Bight of Benin. Exhaustion, hunger, thirst, and the ire of local chieftains threatened to claim his life at several points, but in December he at last reached Badagry. There, new items were added to the catalog of horrors he had endured. One night, two wives of the ruler were executed "for having spoken their mind with too much frankness" and were suspended from the branches of a tree outside his hut; on another occasion, while exploring the environs, Lander came across a "fetish tree," its branches blackened by vultures who tore at and gobbled the rotting flesh off the skeletons of hundreds of individuals who had been sacrificed on that spot to the local deities. A huge mound of skulls had been piled around the tree's trunk; Lander fainted at the sight and had to be revived by his attendant.

But otherwise Lander abided by his friend and master's wisdom. His presence at Badagry was a great irritant to the Portuguese slave traders of the port, who were suspicious of any Englishman's motives and convinced the ruler of the town that Lander was conspiring against him. (England was at the time engaged in initiatives to halt the slave trade, and Lander in fact considered the Portuguese peddlers of human flesh at Badagry the most "evil and barbarous" people he had yet encountered.) The explorer was then summoned to the king's presence, where, he later wrote, "one of the men presented me with a bowl, in which was about a quart of a liquid much resembling water and commanded me to drink it, saying 'If you come to do bad, it will kill you, but if not it cannot hurt you.'" The explorer unhesitatingly quaffed the poison, which his tormentors assured him was invariably fatal, then hastened to his hut, where with the aid of warm water and an emetic from his store of medicines he was able to purge it from his system and by dint of his very survival win the admiration of his hitherto unfriendly hosts. Soon thereafter an English ship called at Badagry and Lander was on his way home.

Lander's counterpart in the exploration of the Niger was much less fortunate, although he did succeed in his dubious ambition of becoming the first European explorer to reach Timbuktu. Laing had made his way toward the Niger and its fabled city via Ghudamis, a Saharan oasis at the juncture

Lander is forced to drink poison in a "fetish hut" at Badagry. His survival of the ordeal greatly impressed the chief there but did not place him out of danger; he "was advised by the king," he wrote, "never to go out unarmed, as the Portuguese took no pains to conceal their inveterate dislike to me; and would no doubt assassinate me the first opportunity that might present itself."

of the present-day borders of Libya, Algeria, and Tunisia and then southwestward across the desert with a Moorish camel caravan through the heart of what are now the nations of Algeria and Mali. Letters sent to Warrington via messenger expressed his love for Emma and his desperation to reach Timbuktu ahead of Clapperton, whose objectives he assumed to be the same as his own, but 100 miles from the city he was set upon by Tuareg nomads as he slept. The attack left him bloodied and scarred from gunshot and sword wounds; his jaw was broken, his right hand nearly severed, and much of one ear lopped off, but he entered Timbuktu on camelback nonetheless on August 18, 1826. (Clapperton and Lander were several hundred miles away to the southeast, convalescing at Kano.) Unfortunately, his impressions of the city remain unknown, for after a stay of little more than a month, he was murdered—apparently because he refused to convert to Islam—by some Tuaregs as he made his departure for the north. His corpse was cast unburied onto the desert sands, where it fed the vultures and ravens.

The precise manner of Laing's demise was discovered by the 27-year-old Frenchman, René Caillié, who a year later became the first European to visit Timbuktu and live to tell about it. Caillié was the almost completely self-educated son of a drunken, thieving baker who died in prison when the boy was nine. Two years later, his mother also passed on, leaving him an orphan. An uncle succeeded in gaining young René an apprenticeship to a shoemaker, but by that time the boy, inspired by his immense enjoyment of Daniel Defoe's great novel about an island castaway, *Robinson Crusoe*, was unwilling to devote his attention to anything but the "reading of voyages and travels."

"I already felt an ambition to make myself famous by some important discovery," Caillié later wrote. "Geographical books and maps were lent to me: the map of Africa, in which I scarcely saw any but countries marked as desert or unknown, excited my attention more than any

In Arab mufti, the French explorer René Caillié takes notes while pretending to study the Koran. Caillié was the first European to visit the fabled city of Timbuktu and live to tell about it.

other." When he was 17, Caillié, having secured a position as an officer's servant, arrived in Senegal in West Africa, where he spent most of the next 10 years, participating in various expeditions, learning Arabic, training himself to navigate and measure distance without the scientific instruments that he would never be able to afford, and generally preparing himself to mount an expedition to Timbuktu.

By April 1827 he was ready, and he set off from the mouth of the Rio Nunez in present-day Guinea in a caravan consisting of himself and 11 African porters, camel handlers, and guides. Caillié himself was in disguise; in order to protect himself from the customary enmity of the peoples of the interior for Europeans and Christians, he dressed in Arab garb and presented himself as an Egyptian by birth who had been taken to France as a young man and just recently released in Sierra Leone. Now, his story went, he was eager to make his way back to the Egypt of his youth and reacquaint himself with the tenets of Islam. He carried with him the Koran, which he made a great display of studying each night; in reality he was jotting down notes about his travels in its margins and on blank pages.

The journey proved difficult and long, taking Caillié over tortuous slopes, through boggy marshes, and across flooded plains. Like those who had gone before him, Caillié soon fell victim to fever, to which were added new torments: a parasite burrowed into his bloodstream through the sole of his foot, causing grotesque swelling and a putrid sore and blister, and scurvy greatly weakened him and caused the roof of his mouth to disintegrate, so that he often wound up spitting out pieces of his jawbone while he ate. He persisted nevertheless, reaching Djenne overland in mid-March 1828 and Timbuktu itself, via canoe on the Bani and then the Niger, scarcely more than a month later. He entered the "mysterious city" with "an indescribable feeling of satisfaction" just as the sun was lowering beneath the horizon, but daylight and a clearer view brought with it something of disillusionment:

> I looked around and found that the sight before me did not answer my expectations of Timbuktu. The city presented, at first view, nothing but a mass of ill-looking houses, built of earth. Nothing was to be seen in all directions but immense plains of quicksand of a yellowish white color. The sky was a pale red as far as the horizon; all nature wore a dreary aspect, and the most profound silence prevailed; not even the warbling of a bird was to be heard. . . . [Timbuktu] is situated in an immense plain of white sand, having no vegetation but stunted trees and shrubs. It may contain at most ten or twelve thousand inhabitants.

Still, though its legendary gold trade was a thing of the past—the city's most important commerce was now in salt—Timbuktu still retained a certain mysterious glamor. "Though I cannot account for the impression," Caillié wrote, "there was something imposing in the aspect of a great city, raised in the midst of sands, and the difficulties surmounted by its founders cannot fail to raise admiration." Less admirable, as Caillié discovered, were the methods used by Laing's assassins: "One of the murderers tied a turban round the neck of his victim and strangled him on the spot, he pulling one end while his comrade held the other."

Unlike the unfortunate Laing, Caillié returned to his homeland to tell his tale, but in the end he suffered what is, for the explorer, a fate perhaps even worse than death. After a horrendous journey northward across the Sahara, in the course of which he suffered the ceaseless torment of unslaked thirst and almost died after being thrown from a camel, he staggered, clad in rags, emaciated, and virtually

Timbuktu's glory days were long past by the time Caillié reached it in March 1828. Though still important as a trade depot for many of the nomadic peoples of the Sahara, it was no longer a major cultural center, as it had been under the Songhai Empire in the 15th and 16th centuries.

delirious, into the French consulate in the Moroccan city of Tangier on September 7. "I am a Frenchman; I have been to Timbuktu," he gasped to the incredulous diplomat who greeted him there, only to hear the man direct his servants to "throw out this dog of a beggar." Repeated visits over the next several days convinced the diplomat of his tale, however, and the appropriate charity was extended; after a brief period of recuperation Caillié was returned to France aboard a ship of his nation. There, though he was awarded the prize offered by the Paris Geographical Society to the first Frenchman to reach Timbuktu, his story was mostly disbelieved, and when he died from consumption at the age of 38 he was still bitter about the skepticism with which his achievements had met. "I must admit," he wrote in his *Travels Through Central Africa to Timbuctoo*, "that these unjust attacks have affected me more deeply than all the hardships, fatigues and privations which I have encountered in the interior of Africa."

Vindication for Caillié came nearly 20 years too late, in 1855, when the German-born explorer Heinrich Barth emerged from Africa, having spent the last 5 years traversing the continent for the British government from Tripoli south to Lake Chad and beyond, then westward to Timbuktu and back to the Mediterranean. Besides confirming Caillié's assertions, Barth personally covered an unprecedented amount of African territory and succeeded, in his *Travels and Discoveries in North and Central Africa*, in presenting the most comprehensive and sympathetic account of the continent, its peoples, its culture, and its history to that point.

But Barth, for all the magnitude of his achievement, solved none of the great geographic mysteries of Africa. Several of these outlived his sojourn on the continent, while the question of the precise location of the terminus of the Niger—the mouth of the great water—had already been solved by two contemporaries of Caillié's. Richard Lander returned to Africa, charged by John Barrow and the

John Lander accompanied his older brother Richard on his second Niger expedition. "I should particularly wish, if there be no objection to it, that my brother John Lander, may be permitted to accompany me, as a companion on my lonely journey," Richard Lander asked John Barrow by letter while the expedition was in its planning stages. As John Lander did not ask to be paid for his services, Barrow had no objection.

British colonial office with resolving the riddle of the Niger, just a scant 18 months after arriving in England following the tragic final Clapperton expedition. He was accompanied to Badagry this time by his younger brother John, an aspiring journalist who shared his fascination with travel if not necessarily his unflagging good humor and stamina. The younger Lander was a more talented writer than his brother, however, and was of a more studious nature, qualities that proved most useful when it came to compiling the narratives by which 19th-century adventurers staked their claims to recognition.

Accompanied by a small retinue of retainers and attendants, the Landers traveled inland from Badagry to the Niger at Bussa between March 31 and June 17, 1831, along a route similar to that taken by Clapperton on his ill-fated last expedition. In the course of their journey, Richard Lander reacquainted himself with such figures from the previous expedition as Adele, king of "the abominable place of Badagry," who had scheduled a mass sacrifice of 300 people—men, women, and children—for shortly after their arrival, and the widow Zuma. To allay the suspicions

"Everything was silent and solitary; no sound could be distinguished save our own voices and the plashing of the paddles with their echoes; the song of birds was not heard, nor could any animal whatever be seen; the banks seemed to be entirely deserted, and the magnificent Niger to be slumbering in its own grandeur."
Thus the Landers described the final days of their voyage to the mouth of the Great Water.

of the native inhabitants regarding their intentions, the Landers claimed to be in search of any surviving personal effects of the late Mungo Park; upriver from Bussa, the explorers were presented with a book, salvaged from the Niger and carefully preserved and protected inside a white cotton cloth, that had belonged to the drowned Scotsman. Hopeful that it might be a lost journal, the explorers were

disappointed to discover that the volume was in fact a table of logarithms.

Though the landscape along the river was often breathtaking—"beautiful, spreading, and spiry trees adorned the country, on each side of the river, like a park; corn, nearly ripened, waved over the water's edge; large, open villages appeared every half-hour; and herds of spotted cattle were observed grazing and enjoying the cool of the shade," John Lander wrote—further disappointments were in store. Dissatisfied with the usual explorers' gifts of various trinkets—scissors, cheap mirrors, sewing needles, colored cloth, knives, and combs—chieftains along the river were reluctant to provide the Landers with the canoe they wanted in order to travel downriver to the Niger's mouth. At last, in two pilfered crafts and then a larger, though leaky, boat given them by a potentate who styled himself the King of Dark Water, the Landers began their voyage to the river's mouth. Neither snorting, irate hippopotami, the menacing words and actions of various chieftains, a succession of terrible storms, nor temporary captivity deterred them—though John Lander did later rail in print against being "classed with the most degraded and despicable of mankind [as] slaves in a land of ignorance and barbarism, whose savage natives have treated us with brutality and contempt"—and on November 16, 1831, the Landers' journey (and decades of speculation and searching) came to an end at a town called Brass, on the Nun River channel of the Niger's multicoursed mouth, where "dogs, goats and other animals, run about the dirty streets, half-starved, whose hungry looks can only be exceeded by the famishing appearance of the men, women and children. . . . Many of them are covered with odious boils, and their huts are falling to the ground from neglect and decay."

The Great Water had now been explored along most of its course; though its source remained a mystery, the direction of its current and the location of its terminus did not, even though John Barrow dismissed the Landers' find com-

pletely, claiming that the real Niger was in fact a completely different river. English merchants were more excited and
hailed the Landers' discovery as offering a new opportunity for investment and commerce. MacGregor Laird, a
young Liverpool merchant, expressed a typical point of
view: "The long sought for highway into Central Africa
was at length found. To the merchant it offered a boundless
field for enterprise, to the manufacturer, an extensive
market of goods."

The Landers paid a high price for their explorations.
While working for Laird and a business consortium known
as the African Inland Commercial Company, Richard died
on the African island of Fernando Po in February 1834 from
the effects of a wound suffered as he was trying to establish
a trading post at the confluence of the Niger and the Benue,
a tributary he had "discovered" in the course of his voyage
down the Great Water. His brother followed him to the
grave a few years later, his death coming from the lingering
effects of an illness contracted in the course of his one
African expedition.

Driven by the Devil

With the Niger revealed, the European exploration of Africa now focused on the great river of the eastern part of the continent, the Nile, and specifically on the search for its source, which had been the subject of historical speculation and theorizing since well before the birth of Christ. Writing in the 5th century B.C., Herodotus, the so-called Father of History, called the mysterious territories where the Nile's source supposedly lay "the wild beast region" and concluded that "of the sources of the Nile no one can give any account. It enters Egypt from parts beyond." In the early decades of the 17th century, two Portuguese Jesuits, Jeronimo Lobo and Pedro Paez, separately reached, in present-day Ethiopia, the source of the Blue Nile, the lesser of the two streams that after merging at Khartoum, in the present-day nation of the Sudan, form the Nile proper, but the source of the White Nile remained the object of explorers' quests. The Scotsman James Bruce, in the 1760s, and the Germans John Lewis Burckhardt, Ludwig Krapf, and Johann Rebmann, in the first half of the 19th century, were among those who were tantalized by the riddle of the Nile and set out to unravel the mystery. Magnificent, long-lost temples, ancient emerald mines, and snow-capped mountains on or near the equator—the so-called Mountains of the Moon first mentioned by the Greco-Egyptian geographer Ptolemy in the 2nd century—were some of the wonders charted by these adventurers, but, for all the various claims forwarded, the starting place of the Nile remained unknown.

This portrait of Sir Richard Francis Burton was done in 1876, when the explorer was 55 years old. By that time, wrote a contemporary, his life had known "more of study, more of hardship, and more of successful enterprise and adventure, than would have sufficed to fill up the existence of half a dozen ordinary men."

One thing these early explorers of the Nile did irrefutably demonstrate was the futility of trying to reach its source from the north, as rapids, waterfalls, pest-ridden swamps, and the sheer length of the journey thus required effectively prohibited a successful survey. Consequently, with the reports by Rebmann, Erhardt, and others of the supposed presence in east-central Africa of a huge lake or inland sea in the vicinity of the mysterious snowy mountains, as yet undiscovered by Europeans and styled Lake Nyasa or the Sea of Ujiji, the search for the Nile took as its starting point the east coast of Africa, specifically the island of Zanzibar, a slave market for the Arab world off the coast of the present-day nation of Tanzania. By the 1850s Zanzibar was squalid and disease-ridden, described by Henry Stanley as "a fetid garbage heap; [where] debris of mud houses, sugar cane leavings, orange and banana peelings, make piles which, festering and rotting in the sun, are unsightly to the eye and offensive to the nostril."

It was from this festering hellhole that Richard Burton and John Hanning Speke, two extremely ill matched English army officers sponsored by the Royal Geographical Society, accompanied by 130 porters and 30 donkeys bearing everything from blankets and mosquito nets to umbrellas, carpenters' tools, beads, and bottles of brandy, set off for the interior in August 1857 in search of the source of the Nile, which, Burton's orders read, "it will be your next great object to discover." The two men had served together previously on a disastrous exploratory expedition in Somalia, in the course of which Burton was permanently disfigured by a spear that smashed through his jawbone and emerged from the opposite cheek, Speke was also badly wounded, and the seeds of the rancor that would destroy their relationship were sown.

That adventure and an insatiable yearning for glory were about all that the two men had in common. Speke was the wellborn scion of a country gentleman, a somewhat diffident and proper young man with a penchant for hunting

and travel who even after 10 years in the army in India confessed that he considered himself less a soldier than "a sportsman and traveler." His extensive travels in the Himalayas, India, and Africa had left him nonetheless uninterested in any culture other than his own. Burton's upbringing was much more irregular; the son of a hard-drinking former army officer who thrashed him regularly with a horsewhip, he was raised in various spots on the Continent without benefit of a formal education. At the University of Oxford, his voracious intelligence and eclectic interests first revealed themselves—he would ultimately master 29 foreign languages—but his restlessness and taste for the exotic soon inspired him to abandon his education in favor of the life of a soldier in India, where he distinguished himself as an intelligence officer and researcher of native habits. Proud of his satanic countenance, Burton was a frightening figure to most of his countrymen, who regarded his fascination with other cultures—England was the only country in which he never felt at home, he

An illustration from Burton's First Footsteps in East Africa, his account of his Somalia expedition with Speke, whose belief that the book impugned his fortitude, slighted his contributions, and insulted his literary ability was the root of the animosity that later developed between the two men.

The admiration John Hanning Speke (pictured) initially held for Burton disintegrated under the hardships of their Nile expedition. Burton was to discover, according to the English historian Christopher Hibbert, "that beneath Speke's quiet, amenably tactful demeanor was a character far less docile, a man of relentless ambition who harbored slights until they hardened into ineradicable grievances."

often said—and his penchant for "going native" as unbecoming a British officer and gentleman. Possessed of a Faustian desire for knowledge—he admitted to being "driven by the devil"—Burton made himself an expert in ethnology, archaeology, poetry, and linguistics, and he was fascinated with subjects considered bizarre and even scandalous by the standards of British society. While in India, he wrote a detailed study of homosexual prostitution in Calcutta, and he translated several erotic masterpieces of Eastern cultures into English. His friend Bram Stoker, the author of the gothic novel *Dracula*, once commented that "as [Burton] talked, fancy seemed to run riot in its alluring power; and the whole world of thought seemed to flame with gorgeous colour." Another Irish writer, Frank Harris, said that Burton "would tell stories of Indian philosophy or perverse negro habits of lust and cannibalism, or would listen to descriptions of Chinese cruelty or Russian self-mutilation till the stars paled out. . . . It was the abnormalities and not the divinities of men that fascinated him."

Initially, Speke, who was six years younger than the 37-year-old Burton, revered the older man, but respect turned to disdain in the course of their hellish Nile expedition. Both men were seriously ill for much of the journey from the coast inland to Tabora, where they arrived in November after crossing bog, jungle, plain, and mountain "physically and morally incapacitated for any exertion beyond balancing ourselves on our donkeys." Burton was delirious, suffering hallucinations of demons and headless men, and Speke was scarcely better connected with reality; the servants had taken advantage of the collapse of leadership to decamp in large numbers, many of them overburdened with stolen goods, most of the donkeys had died, nearly all the expedition's scientific instruments had been lost, and its food had rotted in the intense heat and humidity. At night, scorpions and other insects tortured the two Englishmen; the pismire ant, whose mandibles are strong enough to crush a rat, provided a special torment.

Their agony only fed the animosity that each man now openly expressed for the other. Each explorer now regarded his counterpart as insufferably egotistical, and Speke harbored resentments from their earlier expedition, when he believed Burton had imputed cowardice to him for his behavior during an attack by Somali tribesmen and then had failed to give him proper credit for his contributions in his published account of their exploits. While the puritanical Speke abhorred Burton's indulgence in alcohol and drugs and fascination with the sexual practices of the native peoples they encountered, Burton regarded his counterpart as intellectually unequipped to be an explorer—"he was not a linguist . . . nor a man of science, nor an accurate astronomical observer"—and consistently refused his incessant requests to halt the caravan so that he could hunt. Whereas Burton had once regarded Speke as possessing "an uncommonly acute eye for country," he now regarded him as "unfit for any other but a subordinate capacity"; for his part, the once admiring Speke now characterized Burton as a "perfect blackguard" who had "gone to the Devil" under the influence of native customs and unspeakable habits. Still, at Tabora the two put aside their differences sufficiently to nurse one another to a semblance of health and then, at Burton's insistence, continue westward. They had learned along the way that the purported great inland sea was in fact a number of different lakes to the west and north of Tabora, and they considered it likely that one of them was the source of the Nile.

On February 13, 1858, then, from the peak of a slope so steep that Speke's donkey had collapsed and died during the climb, Burton gazed out upon the waters of mountain-rimmed Lake Tanganyika, the second-largest lake in Africa and the second-deepest in the world, which is nestled in a spectacular setting 2,500 feet above sea level in the Great Rift Valley. "Nothing could be more picturesque than this first view of Tanganyika Lake, as it lay in the lap of the mountains, basking in the tropical sunshine," Burton wrote in *The Lake Regions of Central Africa*, one of his several books based on the expedition. "The shores of this vast crevasse appeared doubly beautiful to me after the silent and spectral mangrove-creeks of the East African seaboard, and the melancholy, monotonous experience of desert and jungle scenery, tawny rock and sun-parched plain or rank herbage and flats of black mire." The beauty of the scene was lost on Speke, who was suffering from an infection of the retina that left him virtually blind; a bout with malaria had meanwhile left Burton without the use of his legs, and he had to be carried on a litter everywhere he went.

The explorers settled in at Ujiji, a village on the lake's eastern shore. Speke was dispatched to obtain a canoe with which the lake could be surveyed, while Burton tried to recuperate. When Speke returned empty-handed four weeks later, Burton was irate. He has "done literally nothing," Burton wrote of his comrade, who was now enduring a new agony: during his trip in search of a boat, a black beetle had lodged itself in his ear and begun burrowing its way toward his brain. The determined insect, wrote Speke, "made me almost deaf and ate a hole between that orifice and the nose, so that when I blew it, my ear whistled so audibly that those who heard it laughed." Burton, who had been rendered almost silent by sores that ulcerated his tongue and the inside of his mouth, was not sympathetic. "When my companion had somewhat recovered . . . from the effects of punching in with a pen-knife a beetle which had visited his tympanum," he wrote, "I began seriously to seek some means of exploring the northern head of Tanganyika."

That particular exploration was doomed to disappointment. Burton had learned of a river at the lake's north end, which he was sure was the Nile, but his and Speke's reconnaissance, conducted in two large canoes, revealed that the river flowed south, into the lake, not north and away as the Nile should have done. (The watercourse in question is in fact the Ruzizi and is part of the Congo system.) Disappointed, the explorers repaired to Tabora, where Speke, who had largely recovered, chafed at the inactivity imposed upon him by Burton's need to further convalesce. The poor hunting he had experienced in the course of his trip continued to gall him: "This is a shocking country for sport. There appears to be literally nothing but Elephants, and they from constant hunting are driven clean away from the highways; all I have succeeded in shooting have been a few antelopes and guinea fowls besides hippopotamus near the coast. . . . There is literally nothing to write about in this uninteresting country. . . . Everywhere in fact the country is one vast senseless map of sameness." Lacking Burton's ability to immerse himself in the life of whatever strange place he happened to find himself in, Speke fumed and groused, until at last Burton allowed him to depart on a short expedition to one of the great lakes that supposedly lay to the north. Firmly convinced by now of Speke's essential incompetence, Burton was sure that the younger man's trip would reveal nothing of geographic or scientific value. "To get rid of him" was Burton's succinct subsequent explanation for why he approved Speke's trip; most likely he imagined that the trigger-happy traveler would spend several weeks hunting and then return.

To Burton's eternal regret, Speke claimed the great object of their geographical quest. A relatively easy hike of two weeks northward over wide plains brought him, on August 3, 1858, to the shore of another huge lake, larger, it seemed, even than Tanganyika. He named it Lake Victoria Nyanza—Victoria for the reigning queen of England, Nyanza from the native word meaning great water—and immediately surmised, without further significant reconnaissance, that this gigantic body of water, 250 miles long by 200 miles wide, extending northward, according to one of his native guides, "probably to the end of the world," was the source of the White Nile. At Tabora, to which Speke quickly returned to report his accomplishment, Burton was not amused. He no doubt immediately recognized the

Whereas Speke was uninterested in native peoples and cultures and dismissed them as inferior, Burton was exceedingly curious and eager to immerse himself in ways of life that were foreign to his own experience, and his uninhibited interest in intoxicants and the varieties of human sexuality earned him Speke's disdain. On his part, Burton was contemptuous of Speke's intellectual shallowness and dishonesty.

ramifications of Speke's find as regarded his own prospects for glory—"to be first in such matters is everything, to be second nothing," he once said—and cited to the discoverer the paucity of evidence he had amassed to prove his claim. Though he would subsequently be proven correct, Speke at this point had little more than his own intuition that Lake Victoria was the Nile's source, and as the more scholarly inclined of the two explorers, Burton insisted to Speke on the necessity for more substantial proof of his claim.

At Burton's demand, the two men now returned to Zanzibar. Feverish still, both had to be carried most of the way on litters, with Speke raving deliriously about the injustices he believed Burton had done him and frequently barking and growling like a dog. From Zanzibar the two made their way to Aden, at the southwest tip of the Arabian Peninsula, where a more rapidly recovering Speke took ship for England. Burton remained behind to convalesce further before undertaking the taxing overseas voyage, secure, he believed, with Speke's assurance as a gentleman that he would not present his claim regarding the source of the White Nile to the Royal Geographical Society (RGS) until Burton had returned to England and could accompany him. "I shall not go up to the Royal Geographical Society until you come to the fore and we appear together. Make your mind quite easy about that," Speke told his companion, but when Burton arrived in England in May 1859, he discovered not only that Speke had appeared before the RGS to claim a discovery that objective evidence did not yet support but that his colleague-turned-rival had secured RGS sponsorship and funding for a new expedition, under his own command, to Lake Victoria and down the Nile.

Speke returned to Africa in 1861. His partner in exploration this time was Captain James Grant, a former fellow officer in the Native Bengal Infantry. A quiet and unassuming Scotsman with an interest in the natural sciences and some aptitude as a painter, Grant was a perfect companion for Speke, with whom he shared a passion for big-game hunting. Despite the desertion of all but two of their 115 porters and the severe reduction of rations at times, the two men generally enjoyed the trek from the coast to Tabora, for the hunting was splendid—zebra, antelope, and giraffe fell to the explorers' guns—and the march was overall "an easy affair," according to Speke. By the time they reached Tabora he had pronounced Grant "a very dear friend."

From Tabora, the explorers proceeded to Karague, a kingdom to the west of Lake Victoria in the present-day nation of Uganda, where they were treated most hospitably and took great amusement in the prevailing conception of female beauty, which held heaviness to be the most attractive physical quality in women; those milk-fattened members of the ruler's harem who had grown too large to stand were judged the greatest beauties. The eccentricities of Mutesa, the tall, handsome *kabaka* (king or ruler) of Buganda, farther north, were less benign. The 25-year-old

James Grant replaced Burton as Speke's companion for his second Nile expedition. This engraving of Grant appeared in Speke's account of that journey, Journal of the Discovery of the Source of the Nile.

Mutesa had, at the beginning of his reign, ordered all 30 of his brothers burned at the stake to eliminate them as rivals for the throne, and his courtiers and attendants were regularly beheaded for such offenses as talking too loudly. When Mutesa, whom the imperious Speke had already offended by insisting on sitting in a chair in the king's presence, expressed an interest in the revolvers the explorers carried—Speke had demonstrated their potency by felling four cows with five shots in the kabaka's court-yard—the Englishman made the mistake of presenting him with a rifle. The king immediately ordered a page to take the gun into the courtyard and test it on the first person he saw; shots and a scream were subsequently heard, and the page returned to report that the gun worked very well indeed. Though appalled by such cruelty and by the ha-bitual drunkenness of most of the court, including the queen mother, "fat, fair and forty-five" (as the explorer

Mutesa (center), the king of Buganda, was an especially cruel and capricious potentate whose capacity for random violence made Speke most uneasy. Even so, the two formed an alliance of sorts, with Speke relying on Mutesa's protection while in his kingdom, which the king gladly gave in the hope of obtaining guns from the Englishman.

described her in his published narrative, *Journal of the Discovery of the Source of the Nile*), whom he was appalled to observe regularly on all fours drinking the local beer from a trough "like a pig," Speke soon took to palace life with a gusto Burton would have applauded and secured for himself several mistresses, including a girl named Meri, with whom he had a child.

With gifts from Mutesa of cattle, coffee, and tobacco, the explorers departed Buganda on July 7. Grant was sent ahead to the kingdom of Bunyoro, and on July 21, at Urandogani, 40 miles downstream from Lake Victoria, Speke reached the Nile, which was there "a magnificent stream, from 600 to 700 yards wide, dotted with islets and rocks, the former occupied by fishermen's huts, the latter by terns and crocodiles basking in the sun." Six days' journey upstream brought him at last to the great cataract, named by him Ripon Falls after one of the noble sponsors of the expedition, where the Nile spilled from Lake Victoria and began its more than 2,000-mile journey to the Mediterranean.

Reunited, the explorers reached Gondokoro, a village on the Nile several hundred miles downstream, on February 15, 1863. To their great surprise, they were greeted there by another English explorer, Samuel Baker, who was equally amazed by their arrival and appearance. "All of my men were perfectly mad with excitement," Baker wrote. "Firing salutes, as usual with ball-cartridges, they shot one of my donkeys—a melancholy sacrifice as an offering at the completion of this geographical discovery. . . . Speke appeared the more worn of the two: he was excessively lean, but in reality was in tough condition; he had walked the whole way from Zanzibar, never having once ridden during that wearying march. Grant was in honorable rags. . . . He was looking tired and feverish, but both men had a fire in their eye that showed the spirit that had led them through."

Baker possessed some of that same spirit. Born in the English countryside to a life of wealth and privilege in

Samuel and Florence Baker were one of the few husband-and-wife teams in the history of African exploration. Florence's humble background and irregular (by the standards of Victorian society) relationship with Samuel caused Queen Victoria to snub her at a reception honoring her husband.

1821, he possessed a multitude of gifts—enormous physical strength, the writer's facility with language, the raconteur's gift of gab, a genuine aptitude as a portraitist, an admirable singing voice, a scholar's intellect, and considerable knowledge in the sciences—with no clear conviction of how they might best be employed. In his younger years, he expended his considerable energies as a sportsman, delighting, he said, in "whole hecatombs of slaughter," hunting deer on foot and armed only with a knife in Scotland, and setting a record on the island of Ceylon for the individual slaying of elephants. He led always a footloose life, though not without its accomplishments, but even the founding of an agricultural colony in Ceylon and the construction of a railroad connecting the Danube River to the Black Sea left him dissatisfied, and in 1862 he drifted to Africa from Turkey in search of Speke, accompanied by his redoubtable and beautiful young companion (and later wife), Florence, whom he had rescued from a slave market in Transylvania. "You know that Africa has always been in my head," he informed his family by letter. "I am going to Khartoum, and thence God only knows where, in search of the sources of the Nile." The remarkable couple then made their way from Khartoum to Gondokoro, encountering en route, as Baker put it, "the luxuries of the country as usual . . .

malaria, marshes, mosquitoes, misery; far as the eye can reach, vast treeless marshes perfectly lifeless."

Baker's hope had been to join Speke's expedition while it was still on the verge of accomplishment; the news that his countrymen had already made their find and concluded their explorations left him deeply distressed. "Does not one leaf of the laurel remain to me?" he disappointedly asked Speke, who assured him that there was still work to be done. South of Gondokoro, west of Lake Victoria, Speke told Baker, there was said to lie a body of water called by the natives Luta N'zige. With his usual unerring geographical intuition, Speke speculated that the Nile flowed into this undiscovered lake from Lake Victoria and then northward, and he urged Baker to go in search of it.

So while Speke and Grant proceeded on to Khartoum and then to London with news of their discovery, Baker and Florence continued south. Despite the advice given them in Gondokoro about the country ahead—"you can do nothing without plenty of men and guns"—they were accompanied by just 13 porters, though after reaching the kingdom of Bunyoro their expedition was augmented by

"The Devil's own regiment," on loan from Kamrasi, king of Bunyoro, accompanied the Bakers part of the way to Lake Albert Nyanza. Initially, Kamrasi had said that he would provide Baker with protection only if the explorer gave him Florence in exchange.

At the Murchison Falls, discovered and named by the Bakers in March 1864, the Victoria Nile plunges 120 feet and becomes the Albert Nile. At the foot of the falls, the Bakers' canoe was almost capsized by an angry mother hippopotamus defending her children.

600 warriors dispatched to them by Kamrasi, the realm's monarch. "The Devil's own regiment," Baker called this exotic escort, whose members covered their bodies with leopard and monkey skins, wore antelope horns on their head, and affixed false beards to their chins and cow's tails to their posteriors and amused themselves by plundering villages along the way. With this menacing entourage, the Bakers reached Luta N'zige, which they renamed Lake

Albert Nyanza (Prince Albert was Queen Victoria's husband), on March 14, 1864, and Samuel, "with a heart full of gratitude, . . . drank deeply from the Sources of the Nile." In a masted dugout canoe, the Bakers then sailed eastward out of the lake on the Nile as far as an impassable waterfall, named by them the Murchison Falls, whose deep basin "literally swarm[ed] with crocodiles." As Florence was by now dangerously ill, Samuel, whose own stamina had been exhausted, called a halt, and they began the arduous journey back—to Gondokoro, to Khartoum, and finally to England, where Speke's purported solution to the mystery of the Nile had only unleashed further controversy.

Preceded by his own telegram proclaiming "the Nile is settled," Speke had returned to England in 1863 to accolades, but acclaim soon turned to disillusionment as his arrogant behavior alienated those who had been inclined to support him. Though Speke's theories about the course and sources of the Nile were accurate, his detractors, Burton first among them, were also correct that he had not, by any prevailing standard, mustered the requisite scientific evidence to prove them. He had traced the Nile for no more than 40 miles out of Lake Victoria and thus could not prove, in any real sense, that the watercourse that left the great lake he had discovered was the same one that flowed into Lake Albert and thence northward to Gondokoro and beyond. As Burton put it, Speke had not consistently followed the path of the Nile but rather "marched overland most of the way to Gondokoro and when by chance on the journey he had caught sight of a river . . . any river . . . he had airily concluded that it was the same stream that he had seen issuing from the lake." Speke's potential allies in the RGS were alienated by his refusal, for fear that it would lessen the interest in his forthcoming book on his travels, to write an article about his expedition for the society's journal, and he further outraged them by announcing, without consulting with the society, that he intended to mount a new expedition for the purpose of crossing

Africa from east to west. "Unless I do it," he arrogantly proclaimed, "it will not be done this century."

But his foremost opponent continued to be Burton, who returned to England from a post as consul on the West African island of Fernando Po (present-day Bioko, just off the coast of Cameroon in the Bight of Biafra) in 1864. Despite his position, while there he had concerned himself more with exploration and adventure than with Britain's commercial interests; he had explored the mouth of the Niger, climbed the highest peak in Cameroon, ventured into the jungle in Gabon in search of the elusive lowland gorilla, and sailed up the Congo for a short distance, but he reveled most in his experiences in the "blood-stained land" of Dahomey (a kingdom that is now part of the nation of Benin), where he was sent to investigate reports of human sacrifice. His first visit was disappointingly bloodless—"not a man killed or a fellow tortured . . . at Benin . . . they crucified a fellow in honor of my coming—here nothing," he wrote a friend—but his second sojourn there was more eventful. According to Burton, some 500 individuals, after being given messages to carry to the dead, were executed each year at the king's court, and he was privileged to witness some of the ceremonies. Though he formally protested, in the name of the British government, against the bloodletting, he was an enthusiastic participant in the drinking and celebrating that formed an essential part of the ritual, and he so delighted the king by dancing a few steps with him that the monarch drank a toast in his honor from a human skull.

Back in staid England, Burton pressed his attacks on Speke, disparaging him as a fundamentally unscientific explorer and forwarding his own claim, of which he was now reconvinced, that Lake Tanganyika was the likely source of the Nile. A more compelling public figure than Speke, Burton soon enjoyed much support in the dispute, which was waged in newspapers, books, and journals, even though he had no more evidence than did Speke to back

his argument. Eventually, a public debate between the two rivalrous explorers was scheduled at Bath for September 16, 1864, at the annual conference of the British Association for the Advancement of Science. Though he agreed to appear, Speke did not relish the confrontation; an uninspiring figure, now nearly deaf, he knew that he was likely to come off poorly in comparison with the charismatic Burton and would be unable to defend his claims on a purely scientific basis. On the day before the debate, he was found dead on a relative's property where he had gone to hunt, shot through the chest. "My God, he's killed himself," Burton exclaimed on being given the news, but the coroner ruled the death an accident in the belief that Speke's rifle had inadvertently discharged as he scaled a wall. If so, it was the only shooting accident the great white hunter was ever known to have experienced.

The Bakers' discovery of Lake Albert Nyanza—"a grand expanse of water," wrote Samuel—supported Speke's theory about the source of the Nile. The Victoria Nile flows from Lake Victoria Nyanza to Lake Kyoga and then to the northern end of Lake Albert Nyanza, from where it flows northward on its journey to the Mediterranean. Though Speke had surmised correctly, he feared that he would not be able to prove his contentions in debate with Burton.

Haunted
by Waters

Among the luminaries scheduled to be present at
Bath for the debate between Burton and Speke was the
Scotsman David Livingstone, who had begun his career as
a physician and missionary in South Africa in 1841. A
tireless loner whose character had been tempered by the
14-hour days in a cotton mill he had put in as a boy between
the age of 10 and 18, which were followed by two hours of
school and then more study in the crowded family home,
Livingstone soon grew disillusioned with life at the remote
missions of Kuruman and Mabotsa, where his work was
made difficult by the indifference of the native peoples to
Christianity, the self-satisfaction of his fellow English,
and the outright opposition of the Boers (the Dutch or
Huguenot settlers of South Africa), who enslaved the
peoples he hoped to convert. Accordingly, starting in 1849,
he began to devote the majority of his time and energy to
unraveling the geography of south and central Africa,
much to the distaste of his employers, the London Missionary Society, who regarded his journeys as "only remotely
connected with the spread of the gospel." He crossed the
unforgiving Kalahari Desert three times (once in the company of his wife and three children), traversed the southern
part of the continent westward to the Atlantic at Luanda
(in present-day Angola) through the Kalahari and 1,500
miles of uncharted territory, and discovered breathtaking
Victoria Falls—"the most wonderful sight I had witnessed
in Africa"—and the mighty Zambezi River, the course and

*"In the annals of exploration of
[Africa], we look in vain among
other nationalities for a name such
as Livingstone's," wrote Henry
Stanley about the man he "rescued."
"He stands preeminent above all; he
unites in himself all the best qualities
of other explorers." Unlike many
other explorers of Africa, David
Livingstone (pictured) was remem-
bered fondly by the native peoples
for his great kindness.*

In 1843, two years after he had come to Africa, Livingstone was badly mauled by a lion while working at a mission he had founded at Mabotsa (in the present-day nation of South Africa). The beast crushed his left shoulder and arm, and the injuries troubled him for the rest of his life.

tributaries of which he spent many years exploring. "This was a most important point," Livingstone wrote, "for the river was not previously known to exist there at all," and he immediately regarded it as the waterway whereby "Christianity and commerce" could be used to end slavery on the continent and bring its people to "civilization" through a "long-continued discipline and contact with superior races by commerce." Upon his return to England in 1856 he was lauded by Sir Roderick Murchison of the RGS for having achieved "the greatest triumph in geographical research . . . in our times," and the public hailed him as a hero.

After resigning from the London Missionary Society, Livingstone returned to Africa in 1859 with the grand title of Her Majesty's Consul for East Africa and an even grander scheme for navigating the Zambezi by steamship to demonstrate its worthiness as an inland commercial highway and its potential as a site for trading posts and missions. Though before he was called back to England in 1863 he drove himself and his men untiringly, covered much territory, and discovered Lake Nyasa, the third-largest such body of water in Africa, the expedition was judged a failure by the British government, for the Zambezi and its most important northern tributary proved unnavigable in many places. To the public, Livingstone remained a hero as an explorer and an unyielding opponent of the slave trade, but some of his saintly aura was lost: the Englishmen who had accompanied him found him moody, self-absorbed, sullen, abusive, and prone to violent outbursts of temper, though always charitable, generous, and understanding toward Africans. One of his assistants, Dr. John Kirk, concluded that Livingstone was "one of those sanguine enthusiasts wrapped up in their own schemes whose reason and better judgement is blinded by headstrong passion" and even speculated that he had gone insane.

The Burton-Speke contretemps provided Livingstone with a focus for his next expedition. Though he had no personal knowledge of the geography in question, he did not hesitate to opine that both of the two antagonists were in error about the source of the Nile. Burton, he said, was a "beastly fellow" and a "moral idiot" whose behavior could not "be spoken of without disgust," while Speke was "a poor misguided thing" of "slender mental abilities" who had "turned his back upon the real source of the Nile." The Nile, claimed Livingstone, actually originated in neither Lake Victoria nor Lake Tanganyika, but far south of the lake in largely unknown bodies of water.

So in March 1866 Livingstone returned to Africa to prove his theory and document further the horrors of the Arab slave trade. His last expedition began from Zanzibar and took him first, in five agonizing months, along the Rovuma River to the southern shore of Lake Nyasa, by which time virtually all of his attendants had deserted and most of the camels, buffaloes, and mules he had brought as beasts of burden had been felled by the dreaded tsetse fly. Livingstone himself was suffering terribly in the "steaming, smothering air" and "dank, rank, luxurious vegetation" through which the expedition passed. Though plagued by dysentery, rheumatic fever, and ulcers on his feet, he continued onward to the northwest, across the Muchinga Mountains to lakes Mweru and Bangweulu, traveling through "dripping forests and oozing bogs," often in mud up to his neck. His health was rapidly failing; deserting servants had made off with his medicine chest, and Livingstone, often incoherent, recorded in his diary his dismay at being "hardly [able] to keep up with the march, though formerly I was always first." During the mountain passage he suffered "from real hunger and fainting," and he was obliged to take in his belt three notches. "Every step jars on the chest," he wrote, "and I am very weak." At Zanzibar, some of the deserted servants spread the false news that Livingstone and all of his party had been killed. The explorer, meanwhile, was making his way to Ujiji, on the eastern shore of Lake Tanganyika, where he hoped to obtain medical supplies and provisions, regain some measure of health, and then march to the Lualaba River, which, joined by the Luapula River from Lake Mweru, he believed then fed the Nile. The trek to Ujiji, which he reached on March 14, 1869, was his most hellish episode yet; he contracted pneumonia and hallucinated constantly, seeing spirits and the faces of individuals revealed to him in the bark of trees.

In the meantime, the plight of the world-famous Livingstone was the subject of much speculation in the outside world. The report of his death was quickly debunked, but various sensational rumors about his possible fate continued to circulate, and the theory that he was likely in some need of rescue soon held sway. Recognizing the depth of the public curiosity about this matter, the younger James Gordon Bennett, the enterprising publisher of the *New York Herald*, dispatched one of his best correspondents, a young man named Henry Morton Stanley, to search for the missing explorer. "Go and find him wherever you may hear that he is, and get what news you can of him," Stanley was

(*continued on page 89*)

Tribal Cries and Tsetse Flies

Richard Burton, pictured here in Arab dress, was in many ways ideally suited for the hardships of Africa, but he was no more immune than other explorers before him to the continent's diseases.

The Europeans who in the 18th and 19th centuries explored the uncharted interior of Africa willingly subjected themselves to some of the harshest environments and circumstances known to man. Perhaps only the first American and European explorers of North America encountered a landscape as richly endowed with such a variety of flora and fauna, but though exploration in North America was often perilous, the environment through which the continent's discoverers moved was not itself inherently threatening to health; some scholars now believe that infectious diseases were all but unknown in North America prior to the arrival of Europeans, and, indeed, it was the newcomers themselves, as the carriers and spreaders of new germs and viruses, who posed the greatest threat to the human life of the New World. In Africa, the situation was reversed; in addition to the perils posed by wild animals and native peoples displeased by the prospect of European colonization, explorers and traders experienced a bewildering array of ailments. The air itself seemed to carry pestilence and fever: in Africa Europeans seemed to die from the rain, from the heat, from mysterious vapors and miasmas born in the continent's bogs and steamy jungles. In actuality, the killers were most often a trio of deadly, mostly unseen, entities—the tsetse fly, the anopheles mosquito, and the water snail, carriers of sleeping sickness, malaria, and bilharzia. Though other, more picturesque dangers more greatly interested the readers who eagerly snapped up explorers' African narratives, in truth it was these three pestiferous assassins who transformed the continent into the "white man's grave."

Africa is often envisioned as a land of dense and steamy jungles, but huge swaths of desert lie across the north and south. Desert crossings provided many perils, not the least of which were Arab slave traders who often took pleasure in torturing Christians in the name of their god, Allah. Many explorers adopted Muslim dress and habits before setting out.

Thomas Baines painted this scene of David Livingstone's
men firing from the Ma-Robert on an elephant in the
Shoe River. Though Livingstone tried to be gentle with
Africa's inhabitants and sparing with its animals, he was
often forced to defend his life—he was once mauled by a
lion near Mabotsa, and though he escaped he never fully

When Livingstone discovered that the Zambezi and its tributaries originated in central Africa, he thought that he had found the route by which "Christianity and commerce" could reach the African interior, but upon hearing the reports of swampy plains, gummy bogs, and dramatic cataracts, his European sponsors believed the river to be unnavigable.

Baines's romantic rendition of the Victoria Falls, which Livingstone happened upon and named in November 1855. Baines painted buffalo stampeding toward the falls, but Livingstone records that although the area was full of game, they were "all very tame."

Enraged warriors mourn the death of a fellow tribesman. On his trip to Lake Albert, Samuel Baker avoided certain African tribes, infamous for their cruelty and love of war, by traveling with a band of Arab slave traders.

Baker placed his companion (later his wife),
Florence, in the background of this painting.
Florence was a "slight, fair girl," but her
strong constitution enabled her to quickly
adapt to the rigors of East Africa.

Baker, though not a professional artist, was a skilled painter
who was much inspired by his African surroundings. This
warrior from the Commorro tribe is running into battle; his
headdress indicates that he is of a superior rank.

In this painting by Baker, a tethered horse is about to
be gored by a charging rhinoceros. Though vegetarian
in diet and extremely myopic, the rhinoceros will charge
madly at just about anything that excites its sensitive

(continued from page 80)

told. "And perhaps the old man may be in want; take enough with you to help him should he require it. Of course, you will act according to your own plans, and do what you think best—but find Livingstone."

Though he had no African experience, Stanley was in many ways well prepared for his task, for the many adventures he had experienced in his 27 years had made him a most self-reliant individual. Born John Rowlands in Wales to an unwed mother who soon abandoned him, he endured various abuses at a workhouse for foundlings until finally, provoked beyond all endurance, he thrashed the master and ran away. By working a succession of odd jobs, he made his way to the English port of Liverpool where, like countless young men with doubtful prospects before him, he decided to take to the sea and test his fortunes in America. The *Windermere* carried him to New Orleans, where he jumped ship and, blessed for once, was taken in by a kindly merchant named Henry Morton Stanley, whose name he subsequently took. Their relationship was not untroubled, however, and young Stanley frequently ran away from home, returning with fantastic tales of his escapades.

Permanent escape came with the outbreak of the Civil War in 1861. Stanley enlisted in the army of the Confederacy and received his baptism of fire at the bloody Battle of Shiloh in April 1862, where he was taken prisoner by the Union forces. After a brief subsequent stint in the Union navy, Stanley deserted and lit out for the West, where he obtained a job as a reporter with the *Missouri Democrat*. Journalistic stints in Turkey and covering the Indian wars in the American West followed and helped Stanley land a spot with the prestigious *New York Herald*. After scooping the rest of the world with his account of a British expedition sent to rescue missionaries and soldiers held hostage by the king of Abyssinia, he was given the assignment of locating Dr. Livingstone.

Bennett's deep pockets allowed Stanley to organize one of the largest and best-equipped expeditions ever

Stanley's command style on the trail could not have been more different from Livingstone's. While his fellow Europeans were often appalled that Livingstone treated them so poorly and the Africans so gently, Stanley drove his African charges mercilessly. Here, in an illustration from his book How I Found Livingstone, *he threatens to shoot a native porter if he drops a box while fording a river.*

to penetrate the African interior. Twenty-three heavily armed escorts guarded 157 porters and a couple of dozen beasts of burden as they carried tons of provisions from Bagamoyo, on the coast near Zanzibar, inland to Tabora. Ignoring the warning of the British consul at Zanzibar, John Kirk, that Livingstone in all likelihood did not desire to be rescued, Stanley was similarly self-assured in his treatment of the members of his expedition. Deserters were hunted down and placed in slave chains, and flogging was used to encourage "lazily inclined" bearers to greater efforts. Those who resisted were hanged, but Stanley raised morale by sometimes allowing his party to plunder villages, which, he wrote, seemed to him "an excellent arrangement" in that it "saved trouble of speech, exerted possibly in useless efforts for peace and tedious chatter." Driven unyieldingly, the expedition made the 212 miles from the coast to Tabora in just two months, arriving there in early April 1871.

Wars and continued difficulties with his men slowed Stanley's westward progress at this point, prompting him to confide to his journal that "I do not think I was made for an African explorer, for I detest the land most heartily." Nevertheless, in early November 1871, with an American flag flying at the head of his column, he entered Ujiji. "I pushed back the crowds," he wrote, "and passing from the rear walked down a living avenue of people, till I came in front of a semicircle of Arabs, in front of which stood a white man. . . . As I advanced slowly toward him I noticed he was pale, looked weary, had a grey beard, wore a bluish cap with a faded gold band around it, and had on a red-sleeved waistcoat and a pair of grey tweed trousers. I would have run to him, only I was a coward in the presence of such a mob—would have embraced him, only he being an Englishman, I did not know how he would receive me; so I did what cowardice and false pride suggested was the best thing—walked deliberately to him, took off my hat, and said:

'Dr. Livingstone, I presume?'

An illustration, from Stanley's published account, of his famous meeting with Livingstone at Ujiji. Stanley's detractors found his unpretentious greeting to the famous explorer to be insufficiently eloquent, and "Dr. Livingstone, I presume" soon became a comic catchphrase in London.

'Yes,' said he, with a kind smile, lifting his cap slightly."

Though he indeed did not wish to be rescued, Livingstone was not offended by Stanley's arrival. Just a few months earlier, disheartened by his failure to reach the Lualaba—rains, illness, and the desertion of all but three of his servants had forced him to turn back to Ujiji—Livingstone had written that "all seems against me." A gruesome massacre of their human merchandise by Arab slave traders in the village of Nyangwe, which he witnessed, further depressed him, but he said that Stanley had brought him "new life" and praised his initiative and achievement in reaching him. Though in his diary Stanley acknowledged the darker side of Livingstone's personality, in his articles for the *Herald* (and later his books) he showered him with praise, and he was exceedingly grateful for the affection and goodwill shown him by the older man. "I expected to meet a crusty misanthrope," wrote Stanley, "but I met a sweet opposite, and by leaps and bounds, my admiration grew in consequence." When Livingstone's son Oswell, who was attached to a different rescue expedition dispatched belatedly by the RGS, informed his father that Stanley was going to "make his fortune" off him, Livingstone replied, "If so, he is heartily welcome, for it is a great deal more than I could ever make out of myself."

Though he had found Livingstone, Stanley could not save him. The two men traveled together back to Tabora, but there they parted company—Stanley for England and immense fame, and Livingstone, citing Herodotus and the Old Testament as geographic authorities, back into the interior in continuation of his doomed quest for the Nile's source. In search of the Luapula, which flows from Lake Bangweulu to Lake Mweru, thus feeding the Lualaba and constituting in Livingstone's fatigued mind the true source of the Nile, he exhausted his remaining reservoirs of health and strength, and he was soon being borne on a litter by his eternally faithful servants Susi and Chuma. He died in prayer early on the morning of May 1, 1873, somewhere in the swampy hinterlands north of Lake Bangweulu, suspecting but still unable to admit to himself the unbearable truth that the waterways he was investigating were in fact part of another great river system—the Congo—rather than the Nile. "Nothing earthly will ever make me give up my work in despair," he wrote in his journal. "I encourage myself in the Lord my God and go forward."

In England, meanwhile, Stanley was reaping the dubious benefits of fame, sought after by the public for lectures and appearances and hyped by the *Herald* as one of the greatest African travelers of the day. Still, his exploits were questioned by no small amount of naysayers, who correctly pointed out that Stanley had added no new geographical knowledge and lampooned what they regarded as the fatuousness of his famous greeting to Livingstone. Annoyed that an American reporter should have beat its representatives to Livingstone, the RGS was especially snippy; Stanley's admittedly ill prepared speech to them was received with a frosty silence, and he left "in great indignation" the subsequent dinner given in his honor. Even in the United States, his adopted homeland, where the eminent writer Mark Twain compared his achievement to Columbus's, there were those who echoed the English press's claim that he was a charlatan and his story nothing more than an elaborate hoax. A prickly personality at best, always sensitive to slights, Stanley took little solace in his laurels, and he was unable to forget the insults. Determined to silence his critics, he proposed and organized, with the sponsorship of the *New York Herald* and the London *Daily Telegraph*, the most ambitious African expedition yet conceived—the exploration of lakes Victoria and Albert and the wilderness beyond for the purpose, so he thought, of dispelling Speke's claims regarding the Nile and proving Livingstone's.

At Zanzibar, where in late 1874 Stanley assembled some 400 Africans who would accompany him and his three English companions, Frederick Barker and the brothers

This photograph, the most famous portrait of Stanley, captures the explorer as he appeared in 1872, having just achieved fame for his success in finding Livingstone.

Francis and Edward Pocock, to the interior, he anticipated the dispiriting inevitable course that his expedition, like all those that had gone before him, would take: "The magnificent caravan which started from the sea 400 strong, armed to the teeth, comfortable, well laden and rich, each armed man strong, healthy, well chosen, his skin shining like brown satin, eyes all aglow with pride and excitement . . . twelve stately, tall guides, tricked out in crimson joho and long plumes, heading the procession . . . while brazen trumpets blow and blare through the forest. Ah! This was a scene worth seeing. But three weeks from now how different will be the greatly diminished caravan. Scores will have deserted, the strong will have become weak, the robust sick, the leader will be ready to despair and to wish that he had never ventured a second time into the sea of mishaps and troubles which beset the traveller in Africa!"

Stanley was mistaken only as to the timing, for after three weeks the expedition was still intact, but by the time it

More than any African explorer before him, Stanley relied on the advantage in firepower given him by modern weaponry rather than peaceful parleys with the native inhabitants of the territories he passed through. The illustration is from a late-19th-century book about Stanley's exploits.

reached Lake Victoria in February 1875 after weeks of travel on a "narrow, ill-defined track" among "a labyrinth of elephant and rhinoceros trails," disease ("the dreadful scourge of the expedition has been dysentery"), desertion, hunger, and warfare—Stanley proved noticeably less reluctant than any African explorer before him to engage native peoples militarily—had taken their usual toll, and the expedition was down to 169 men. Undaunted by "strange tales about the countries on the shores . . . one man reports a country peopled with dwarfs, another with giants, and another is said to possess a breed of such large dogs that even my mastiffs are said to have been small compared to them," he and Frank Pocock circumnavigated the lake in the *Lady Alice*, a 40-foot collapsible boat designed by Stanley and named by him after his fiancée. His survey demonstrated, as Speke had earlier surmised, that Lake Victoria Nyanza was in fact the source of one branch of the Nile, and a similar subsequent reconnaissance of Lake Tanganyika, conducted after a brief intervening excursion to Lake Albert, proved the impossibility of Burton's claims regarding it.

Stanley now set out to test Livingstone's theories by following the Lualaba and its related waterways to their outlet on the sea. When he left Nyangwe—the farthest point in the interior reached by Livingstone and the deepest post in the interior known by Europeans—in November 1876, Stanley did not even know whether his journey would culminate at the Mediterranean or the Atlantic, for the waterways he proposed to follow were completely uncharted. He and Frank Pocock (the other two Englishmen having died) were now accompanied by the remnants of the original expedition plus 700 men loyal to Tippoo Tibb, a half-Arab, half-African slave trader of fearsome reputation, who provided their services in exchange for a hefty payment of goods and money.

Beyond Nyangwe, wrote Stanley, "the largest half of Africa [was] one wide enormous blank . . . a region of fable and mystery . . . a continent of dwarfs and cannibals through which the great river flowed on its unfulfilled mission to the Atlantic." He and his men followed the Lualaba—most of them by land, but some aboard the *Lady Alice* where the river was navigable—through equatorial jungle so thick that even at noon the journalist-turned-explorer found it too dark to read his notes without the aid of a torch. Even so, as he would throughout his unprecedented journey, Stanley managed to scrupulously record precise geographic measurements of the regions that he passed through. Two hundred miles north of Nyangwe, Tippoo Tibb turned back with his men; Stanley carried on, urging his dwindling party up the sides of sheer ravines, past raging cataracts, over deserted plains eerily shrouded in impenetrable mist, through the ever deepening jungle. Even when nature seemed to present its most pleasing face, Stanley learned, menace lurked within: "Nature here is either remarkably or savagely beautiful," he wrote at one point. "Overall she has flung a robe of varying green; the hills and ridges are blooming, the valleys and basins exhale perfume; the rocks wear garlands of creepers. . . . Look closer and analyze all this, that you may find how deceptive is distance. The grasses are coarse and high and thick. Their spearlike blades wound like knives and their points like needles; the reeds are tall and tough as bamboo; these pretty looking bushes are thorns. . . and truly the thorns are hooks of steel." The thick growth along the river also hid various human inhabitants, with whom Stanley, in stark contrast to Livingstone—"he was so gentle and patient and told us such pleasant stories of the wonderful land of the white man" some natives told the newcomers about the man they had known as Daoud—proved always willing to do battle rather than engage in what he termed the usual "soft soap" or "sugar and honey" negotiations. His account of the journey becomes at times a virtual litany of skirmishes and ambushes. Although almost always outnumbered, Stanley's forces invariably prevailed by virtue of

Stanley found that in Africa nature often took on a sinister aspect; the fecundity of the jungle overwhelmed the explorers.

their superior firepower—they had guns, and the natives did not.

A victory in battle at one village enabled Stanley to procure enough canoes to transport his entire party on the river, the tremendous power of which made for swift transit, although frequent portages were necessary to avoid its many rapids and waterfalls. Below a series of seven precipitous cataracts known today as the Stanley Falls, their discoverer took a series of altitudinal measurements that revealed incontrovertibly, as he had suspected now for some time, that the river was not the Nile or one of its tributaries but the uncharted Congo. (The Lualaba becomes the Congo below its confluence with the Luapula, in southeast Zaire just north of the city of Manono.) Ahead lay 1,000 miles of unobstructed sailing, and as the *Lady Alice* and the canoes hurtled seaward Stanley was moved to describe the Congo, with its powerful current, as the "Amazon of Africa." The more gentle and sluggish Nile he likened to the winding Mississippi; "the Congo," he wrote, "could furnish water for three Niles," and he praised its potential for trade.

The smooth sailing ended in March 1877, about 450 miles from the river's mouth, just above the present-day cities of Brazzaville and Kinshasha, where the boats had to be guided through raging rapids with ropes manipulated by men on the shores. Below the rapids the river calmed and widened beneath high white cliffs—a section the explorer named Stanley Pool—before turning rough again as it coursed through the ravines of the Crystal Mountains, where Frank Pocock and 11 others were drowned when their canoe overturned as they were trying to navigate one of the 32 cataracts that Stanley dubbed collectively the Livingstone Falls. Beyond the rapids, the *Lady Alice* was abandoned on a clifftop and the canoes were scuttled as the ragged, emaciated band, many of its members on the verge of starvation, made the last of its 5,000 miles to the Atlantic Coast on foot. When they reached the city of Boma in August 1877, Stanley and the approximately 82 others, including 12 women, who had started out 999 days earlier from Zanzibar had completed the greatest journey of African exploration and become the first to cross the continent from the Indian to the African Ocean. In the process they had explored the last of the continent's great rivers to be charted and enabled the world's cartographers to subsequently sketch, in broad outline, the geography and topography of the interior of the continent. Stanley was often and justly criticized for his brutality toward the native peoples of Africa, but this time none could deny the significance of his exploratory efforts.

Though there was still exploration to be done in Africa, in its broadest contours the continent was now known, and in the wake of Stanley's epic transcontinental journey the European nations slowly but inexorably shifted their focus there from exploration to colonization. The race was on among the European nations to claim colonies—in Africa and around the world—from which to extract precious metals, raw materials for their burgeoning industries, and foodstuffs and which could serve as strategic bulwarks against the imperial ambitions of their neighbors and rivals. Whereas in 1870 only a few small, isolated African coastal regions had been claimed as colonies, by 1914 the entire continent had been carved up among Great Britain, France, Germany, Belgium, Portugal, and Spain. Of the various African nations and kingdoms, only Liberia and Ethiopia retained their independence.

Though colonization did create some opportunities for the foremost African explorer of his day—between 1879 and 1884 Stanley worked for the king of Belgium, Leopold, in the so-called Belgian Free State (known later as the Belgian Congo and then Zaire), establishing trading posts along the great river he had explored and inducing various tribal chieftains to relinquish their sovereignty to the Belgian monarch—the great days of geographical exploration in Africa were drawing to a close. In Africa, the transition from modest expeditions led by lonely, visionary travelers to well-financed military expeditions was well under way, and there were no more populated continents for Europeans to explore. "Henceforth," according to the historian Ian Smith, "expeditions were either organized and dispatched by governments, or their agents, with military support for openly political ends; or they were sent by geographical and scientific bodies, often amidst great popular interest, to pioneer trends across inhospitable tracts of the Arctic and Antarctic."

Stanley's last expedition was equal parts nightmare and farce. In 1887, he was dispatched to the rescue of the self-styled Emin Pasha, a German physician and explorer by the true name of Eduard Schnitzer who had been established as governor of Equatoria, the southernmost province of the Sudan, by the British general George "Chinese" Gordon. The Sudan was then nominally under the control of the Egyptian government, which depended on British military might to maintain order there. When Gordon's garrison at Khartoum was overrun by the rebellious forces of the so-called Mahdi, a self-proclaimed prophet of Islam, Emin Pasha was left, according to the European press, menaced and isolated at his stronghold at Wadelai, on the Nile just north of Lake Albert.

At the head of 708 men—the largest expedition ever taken into Africa—Stanley traveled upriver on the Congo

In the course of his mission to rescue the Emin Pasha, Stanley became the first white man to cross the Ituri rain forest; the journey constituted the single most horrific experience of his years of African exploration.

from its mouth to Yambuya, on the Aruwimi, its tributary. From there he set off overland through the Ituri rain forest, a suffocating jungle that he deemed "a region of horrors . . . the blackest nightmare of all my experiences on the Dark Continent." In danger of disintegration already because of the resentment caused by Stanley's imperious command style, the expedition further deteriorated in the rain forest. Stanley tried to capture the gruesome unreality of that grim march in *In Darkest Africa*, his account of the expedition: "Imagine this forest and jungle in all stages of decay and growth . . . old trees falling, leaning perilously over, fallen prostrate; ants and insects of all kinds, sizes, and colors murmuring around; monkeys and chimpanzees above, queer noises of birds and animals, crashes in the jungle as troops of elephants rush away; dwarfs with poisoned arrows securely hidden behind some buttress or in some dark recess; strong, brown bodied aborigines with terribly sharp spears, standing poised, still as dead stumps; rain pattering down on you every other day in the year; an impure atmosphere, with its dread consequences, fever and dysentery; gloom throughout the day, and darkness almost palpable throughout the night . . . you will have a fair idea of the inconveniences endured by us from June 28 to December 5, 1887." Of the 389 men who entered the forest with Stanley—a rear guard was left behind—only 174 emerged. Some of these had resorted to cannibalism to survive. At one point, Stanley left behind a detachment of 52 men, all of them starving or ill, in the care of one of his officers, who had been reduced to a "decrepit skeleton [covered in] a mass of blisters"; within three days 47 of them were dead. The expedition's leader, meanwhile, maintained his usual ironfisted discipline, with corporal punishment imposed for even the smallest transgressions; one unfortunate was hanged for stealing a rifle.

To make matters worse, upon reaching Lake Albert in early 1888, Stanley found the "cordial . . . well-read . . . and quite likeable" Emin Pasha quite unthreatened by the

Mahdi's forces and, like Livingstone before him, with no special desire to be rescued. Leaving the German to ruminate further, Stanley reentered the rain forest in search of his missing rear guard, which he found in disarray, its white commander having been murdered for his outrageous provocations of his black charges and just 98 of its 258 members still alive. Still more died, from smallpox, dysentery, starvation, and poisoned pygmy arrows, as the ragged party made its way back to Lake Albert. En route, Stanley glimpsed—becoming the first European to do so—the fog-shrouded Ruwenzori Range, the mysterious Mountains of the Moon that had to that point eluded the observation of the few European travelers in the region. Convinced finally by Stanley's thunderous fulminations—"I leave you to God," he shouted at one point, "and the blood which will now flow must fall upon your own head"—Emin Pasha decided to leave with him, and the explorer, the governor, and their respective retinues decamped to the east and

A typical Stanley adventure on the way to save the Emin Pasha: "As the boat was crossing the creek, a body of natives had suddenly issued from the bush on the other side and shot their arrows at the crew." (From Stanley's In Darkest Africa, *his account of the Emin Pasha expedition.)*

Bagamoyo, which they reached in December 1889. Stanley had now crossed the continent again, this time from west to east. At Bagamoyo, safe from the clutches of the dreaded Mahdi, the Emin Pasha fell from a balcony while entertaining diplomats from Zanzibar, splitting his skull open but escaping with his life when a zinc shed broke his fall. Stanley was celebrated once again, for his geographical work and his undeniable courage and drive, and condemned, for his brutality and the farcical aspects of the Emin Pasha's rescue. And thus the great age of African exploration drew to a close, fittingly perhaps, on a note of absurdity and waste, to be followed by a new age of interaction between Europeans and Africans, which would itself unfold with often brutal and tragic consequences. Money had been spent, and lives lost, in order to rescue a man who did not want to be rescued, just as much money had been spent, and countless lives lost, in order to discover a continent whose inhabitants were unaware that they or their environs needed to be discovered. "If I were to record all that I saw," wrote Stanley, who spent the remaining 15 years of his life penning narratives and memoirs of his African days, "it would be like stripping the bandages off a vast sloughing ulcer, striated with bleeding arteries, to the public gaze." Despite its racist tinge, MacGregor Laird's observation that "intercourse between civilized and savage nations has hitherto been productive of anything but good to the latter" resonates throughout our century.

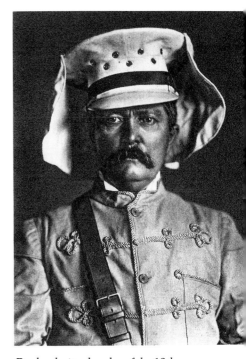

By the closing decades of the 19th century, the European powers were focusing on colonizing the African regions they had explored. Disappointed in England's lack of interest in subduing the Congo, Stanley helped Leopold II, king of Belgium, claim it as his own.

Further Reading

Baker, Samuel. *The Albert Nyanza*. London: Macmillan, 1877.

Boahen, A. Adu. *Britain, The Sahara, and the Western Sudan, 1788–1861*. Oxford: Clarendon Press, 1964.

Bovill, E. W. *The Niger Explored*. London: Oxford University Press, 1968.

Bradnum, Frederick. *The Long Walks*. London: Victor Gollancz, 1969.

Brodie, Fawn. *The Devil Drives*. New York: Norton, 1967.

Burton, Richard Francis. *Lake Regions of Central Africa*. London: Longman, Green, Longman and Roberts, 1860.

Coupland, Reginald. *Livingstone's Last Journey*. London: Collins, 1945.

Davidson, Basil. *The African Slave Trade*. Boston: Little, Brown, 1980.

Farwell, Byron. *Burton*. Holt, Rinehart, & Winston, 1963.

Gibbon, Lewis. *Niger, The Life of Mungo Park*. Edinburgh: Porpoise Press, 1930.

Grant, James Augustus. *A Walk Across Africa*. Edinburgh and London: Blackwood & Sons, 1864.

Hall, Richard. *Lovers on the Nile*. London: Collins, 1980.

———. *Stanley*. Boston: Houghton Mifflin, 1975.

Hibbert, Christopher. *Africa Explored*. London: Allen Lane, 1982.

Jeal, Tim. *Livingstone*. London: Heinemann, 1973.

Johnston, H. A. S., and D. J. M. Muffett. *Denham in Bornu*. Pittsburgh: Duquesne University Press, 1973.

Lander, Richard. *Records of Captain Clapperton's Last Expedition to Africa*. London: Henry Colburn and Richard Bentley, 1830.

Lander, Richard, and John Lander. *Niger Journal of Richard and John Lander*. Edited by Robin Hallet, New York: Praeger, 1965.

Lloyd, Christopher. *The Search for the Niger*. London: William Collins Sons, 1973.

Lupton, Kenneth. *Mungo Park: The African Traveller*. Oxford: Oxford University Press, 1979.

McLynn, Frank. *Stanley: The Making of an African Explorer*. London: Constable, 1989.

Moorehead, Alan. *The White Nile*. New York: Vintage Books, 1983.

Park, Mungo. *Travels in the Interior Districts of Africa*. London: Newnes, 1906.

Ramsford, Oliver. *David Livingstone*. London: John Murray, 1978.

Smith, Ian R. *The Emin Pasha Relief Expedition 1886–1890*. Oxford: Clarendon Press, 1972.

Speke, John Hanning. *Journal of the Discovery of the Source of the Nile*. New York: Harper & Brothers, 1864.

———. *What Led to the Discovery of the Source of the Nile*. London: Blackwood & Sons, 1967.

Stanley, Henry Morton. *Autobiography of Henry Stanley*. Edited by Dorothy Stanley. New York: Greenwood Press, 1969.

———. *How I Found Livingstone*. New York: Negro University Press, 1969.

Williams, Harry. *Quest Beyond the Sahara*. London: Robert Hale, 1965.

Chronology

1788	Founding of African Association in London, England
1795	Mungo Park's first expedition in search of the Niger River; Park fails to reach its mouth or Timbuktu
1805	Park's second expedition to the Niger; Park dies at Bussa on the Niger during an attack by local tribesmen
1822–25	Hugh Clapperton, Dixon Denham, and Walter Oudney journey to Bornu and discover Lake Chad
1824–25	Gordon Laing reaches Timbuktu but dies at the hands of stranglers before he can return to tell his tale
1825–28	René Caillié travels to Timbuktu and returns to France, where he is disbelieved
1825	Clapperton's second expedition, which he does not survive
1830–32	Richard Lander reaches the mouth of the Niger
1851	David Livingstone discovers the Zambezi River
1853–56	Livingstone crosses southern Africa from east to west and back again; discovers and names the Victoria Falls
1857–59	Richard Burton and John Hanning Speke search for the source of the Nile; visit Lake Tanganyika; Speke discovers and names Lake Victoria
1860–63	Speke and James Grant travel to Gondokoro to investigate the sources of the Nile
1863–65	Samuel and Florence Baker discover and name Lake Albert
1864	Speke dies, in what is assumed to be a hunting accident, the day before he is supposed to debate Burton about the Nile sources at the annual conference of the British Association for the Advancement of Science
1866	Livingstone searches for the source of the Nile along the headwaters of the Congo; many rumors of his death or distress reach the outside world

1869   The *New York Herald* hires Henry Stanley to find
        Livingstone in Africa

1871   Stanley finds Livingstone in the village of Ujiji, on the
        eastern shore of Lake Tanganyika

1875   The English *Daily Telegraph* and the *New York Herald* spon-
        sor Stanley's exploration of the Congo and its headwaters,
        in the course of which he crosses Africa from east to west

1887–90 Stanley leads the Emin Pasha Relief Expedition to southern
        Sudan, crossing the continent again, this time from west to
        east

Index

Picture Credits

Bettmann/Hulton: p. 62; Courtesy of the Trustees of the British Museum, photo, General Research Division, the New York Public Library, Astor, Lenox & Tilden Foundations: p. 30; Library of Congress: pp. 16 (neg# USZ62-31518), 21, 32, 34 (neg# USZ62-66636), 37, 38, 39, 40, 41, 42, 47, 49, 51 (neg# USZ62-66791), 53, 61, 66, 67, 68, 70, 71, 72, 75, 76, 78, 81, 82–83, 90, 91, 93, 103; Vikki Lieb: p. 28 (map); The Mansell Collection, London: p. 12; From the private collection of David Mills: pp. 100, 102; National Portrait Gallery, London: p. 58; General Research Division, The New York Public Library, Astor, Lenox & Tilden Foundations: pp. 23, 26, 46, 54–55, 94, 97; Royal Geographical Society, London: pp. 84, 85, 86, 87, 88

Steven Sherman is a graduate of Columbia University. He is currently working on his Ph.D. in sociology at SUNY-Binghamton.

William H. Goetzmann holds the Jack S. Blanton, Sr., Chair in History at the University of Texas at Austin, where he has taught for many years. The author of numerous works on American history and exploration, he won the 1967 Pulitzer and Parkman prizes for his *Exploration and Empire: The Role of the Explorer and Scientist in the Winning of the American West, 1800–1900*. With his son William N. Goetzmann, he coauthored *The West of the Imagination*, which received the Carr P. Collins Award in 1986 from the Texas Institute of Letters. His documentary television series of the same name received a blue ribbon in the history category at the American Film and Video Festival held in New York City in 1987. A recent work, *New Lands, New Men: America and the Second Great Age of Discovery*, was published in 1986 to much critical acclaim.

Michael Collins served as command module pilot on the *Apollo 11* space mission, which landed his colleagues Neil Armstrong and Buzz Aldrin on the moon. A graduate of the United States Military Academy, Collins was named an astronaut in 1963. In 1966 he piloted the *Gemini 10* mission, during which he became the third American to walk in space. The author of several books on space exploration, Collins was director of the Smithsonian Institution's National Air and Space Museum from 1971 to 1978 and is a recipient of the Presidential Medal of Freedom.